# HOW TO GET
# PEOPLE to Follow You

**THIRD EDITION**

## Colette Toach

www.ami-bookshop.com

## How to Get People to Follow You
Third Edition

Author: Colette Toach
Graphics & Cover Design: Jessica Toach

**ISBN-13:** 978-1-62664-027-6

**Other formats of this book:**
eBook ISBN: 978-1-62664-117-4
Kindle ISBN: 978-1-62664-135-8
iBook ISBN: 978-1-62664-134-1

Copyright © 2020 by Apostolic Movement International, LLC
All rights reserved
5663 Balboa Ave #416,
San Diego,
California 92111,
United States of America

1st Printing March 2012
2nd Edition May 2016
3rd Edition August 2020

Published by **Apostolic Movement International, LLC**
E-mail Address: admin@ami-bookshop.com
Web Address: www.ami-bookshop.com

All rights reserved under International Copyright Law.
Contents may not be reproduced in whole or in part in any form without the express written consent of the publisher.

Unless specified, all Scripture references taken from the New King James Version®. Copyright © 1982 by Thomas Nelson. Used by permission. All rights reserved.

# Dedication

To my children: Deborah-Anne, Jessica, Rebekah (Ruby) and Michael. For being my first guinea pigs for my lessons on leadership.

To my wonderful husband Craig. For surviving those lessons with me.

# Foreword

I have a confession to make: Having an expressive wife has saved me many lessons in the school of hard knocks!

You see, having a person so willing to graze her knees and bump her head, I was able to learn from her bruises and walk away wiser. This is the very essence of Colette Toach and it is what makes her the best person to write this book.

When she took on this project, I knew that what would come out of it would be pure gold and something that would bless the body of Christ.

Having started this walk at the bottom and risen up to be the leader she is today, there is no other person who could present the truths like she can. Many books have been written by those who are and always have been leaders. They all left one very important part out - what is it like to start out not being a natural born leader?

Now, you can see a balanced, honest, and hard-hitting truth about this area called "leadership" and getting people to follow you.

Anyone who knows Colette, knows that whatever revelation the Lords shows her, no matter how uncomfortable it is, she will point it out and will be ready to help that person overcome. If you can look past your hurt and pride, she will be the one who will take you through to victory.

This brutal honesty is what sets her apart from many out there and why she is the best person to write this book.

So, as you read the pages in this book, you will:

- Be challenged to look at your failures and wrong motivations so you can overcome.
- Live these principles and become a better person all around, if open to the work of the Lord.
- See your short comings, but you will also see a way to change them.
- See that it takes natural and spiritual abilities to make this work.
- Know the path you need to take, the materials you need, and the milestones to look out for along the way.
- Know what stage you are at in your call to be a leader in the body of Christ.

This is not yet another book for leaders to become better leaders. It is far more than that. It is a book for everyone to read, live, and become the leader God is calling them to be.

No matter your age, position, or gender, this book is a powerful tool in your arsenal to help you succeed and be the best leader you can be for the Lord. The rest is up to you... What are you going to do about it?

Craig Toach

Co-Founder
Apostolic Movement International

# Contents

Dedication .................................................................... 3

Foreword ...................................................................... 4

Contents ...................................................................... 6

Part 01: How to Get People to Follow You ................. 12

Chapter 01 – The First Lesson of Leadership ............. 12

    Your First Lesson: What a Leader You Are Not ....... 16

    The Big Question ..................................................... 17

    Why I Qualify to Teach You ...................................... 19

    The Person You Are ................................................. 20

Chapter 02 – Getting Your Boat Into the Water ......... 24

    Three Steps to Remember ...................................... 25

    1. Where Are You Going? ......................................... 26

    2. What to Do When You Get There ........................ 28

    3. What Are Your Capabilities? ................................. 29

Chapter 03 – Planning the Journey ............................ 36

    What Resources Will You Need? ............................. 39

    First Resource - Character Strengths ...................... 41

    Second Resource - Spiritual Strengths ................... 43

    Your Checklist .......................................................... 45

Chapter 04 – Time to Set Sail .................................... 48

    Summary of Chapters 1-3 ....................................... 53

- Chapter 05 – How to Get People to Admire You ........ 56
  - Why People Should Admire You ............................. 58
  - What *Not* to Do ...................................................... 59
  - What to Do ............................................................. 61
- Chapter 06 – Getting People to Follow 101 ................ 72
  - 1. You Do Not Need to Know Everything ............... 73
  - 2. You Do Not Need to Do Everything.................... 77
  - 3. You Need to Keep Your Finger on the Pulse ....... 85
- Chapter 07 – Keeping Those That Follow.................... 94
  - 4. Keep Watch ......................................................... 95
  - 5. Replacing Yourself – Making Leaders................ 105
  - Summary of Points 1-5 ........................................... 120
- Chapter 08 – Winning the Heart of the Public .......... 124
  - 1. The Reality of Who You Are ............................. 125
  - 2. Where the People Are........................................ 133
  - 3. Leading the People Forward ............................. 139
  - The Power of Appreciation ................................... 143
- Chapter 09 – Following the Ark................................. 148
  - Watch the Ark ........................................................ 150
  - You Have Never Been This Way Before ................ 152
  - Do Not Run Ahead of the Ark............................... 154
  - God's Way Is Easy .................................................. 158
- Chapter 10 – Crossing the Jordan ............................. 162
  - Taking Action at the Jordan .................................. 162

A Second Chance .................................................... 165

The Picture Becomes Clearer ................................. 168

Assess Yourself ....................................................... 169

Part 02: Becoming a Person People Want to Follow 174

Chapter 11 – Don't Scuttle Your Ship ........................ 174

Neediness Takes Away Your Goal .......................... 185

Chapter 12 – Becoming Confident ............................ 190

Getting a Reaction ................................................ 191

Be Louder Than the Others .................................. 192

Don't Just Accept Anyone ..................................... 194

Finding Your Mighty Men ...................................... 196

What Kind of Team Do You Want? ....................... 197

Using Your Point of Strength ................................ 201

Chapter 13 – First Stage of Leadership Training: Servanthood ............................................................. 206

How a Leader Is Made .......................................... 206

Launching up the Leadership Ladder ................... 208

The First Stage of Leadership Training ................. 209

The Servant's Heart .............................................. 212

Miraculous Change ............................................... 215

What the First Stage Forges in You ...................... 216

Becoming a New Vessel ....................................... 218

How Do You Know When It Is Over? ..................... 220

- Chapter 14 – Second Stage of Leadership Training: Transformation Through Pressure ............................ 224
  - Pressure for a Purpose ............................................ 228
  - 1. Displacement of Leadership Images ................. 230
  - 2. Removing the Hindrances ................................. 233
  - What the Second Stage Forges in You .................. 237
  - Your Next Step ....................................................... 243
- Chapter 15 – Third Stage of Leadership Training: Taking on the Load ................................................................ 248
  - Taking on the Load of Responsibility .................... 250
  - Your Vision Will Unfold .......................................... 251
  - Testing Time Begins ............................................... 256
  - 1. Your Mountain Experience ................................ 261
  - 2. New DNA From the Father ................................ 263
  - Doing It in His Power ............................................. 266
  - One Final Principle ................................................. 267
  - Why You Will Succeed ............................................ 269
  - Final Prayer ............................................................ 270
  - Calling Forth the Pillars of Fire ............................... 271
- About the Author ......................................................... 274
- Other Books by Colette Toach ..................................... 275
  - The Apostolic Handbook ........................................ 275
  - Practical Prophetic Ministry .................................. 276
  - Persistent Prayer .................................................... 276

    Mentorship 101 ..................................................... 277
Further Recommendations by the Author ................ 277
    AMI Prophetic School: ........................................... 278
    AMI Pastor Teacher School: .................................. 278
    AMI Campus: .......................................................... 279
Reach out! ................................................................. 281
Bibliography ............................................................. 282

PART 01: HOW TO GET PEOPLE TO FOLLOW YOU

CHAPTER 01

# The First Lesson of Leadership

**PART 01: HOW TO GET PEOPLE TO FOLLOW YOU**

# Chapter 01 – The First Lesson of Leadership

I was 13 years old and at a wilderness survival camp. For the first day, we were divided into groups and given specific obstacles to overcome as a team. We were told that depending on how we worked together during these tasks would determine who the leader of the group would be.

I wanted to be the leader more than anything! Away from home and put in a group with kids that I did not know, I felt confident that I had a chance. I gave it my best shot, offering up ideas, suggestions, and motivation to everyone in the group.

I figured that if I could solve the obstacle puzzle first, that my intelligence would give me the prize I was craving. At the end of the day though, I was not the one who was picked as the leader.

I blamed my failure on the teacher who obviously played favorites. I blamed it on the fact that I was not popular and not one of the "beautiful people". I blamed it on the fact that the kids were just part of a clique and I was left out.

The reality of it though was that I was not chosen for a very simple reason: I was not a leader. I might have had many good ideas that day, but it was not me the group followed. They followed the one person who really was a leader and so that was the girl chosen for the job.

Do not think that things are any easier in the Church, because I would have to say they are harder. In school, the army, and at work, you have no choice but to submit to those placed in authority over you. However, when it comes to ministry, the playing field changes completely. We, as believers, can choose who we want to follow.

Just by picking up this book, it is clear that you know exactly what I am talking about. By now, you have also found out that a few good ideas won't get you very far. It is not enough to have passion. It is not enough to be intelligent. It is not even enough to persevere. Obviously, there is something more that you need to become a leader.

## The Missing Ingredient

Obviously, there is a missing ingredient in your life that is blocking people from following you. Well, I invite you on a journey to discover that missing piece. By the time you put this book on your shelf to gather dust, (like so many before it) you would have received something new in your spirit.

The kind of leader that God wants to make you into is more than you have seen in your life so far. The kind of leader that God wants you to be is something greater than just a job position. The Lord Jesus wants to make you into the kind of leader who reflects Him.

Jesus was radical, ambitious, passionate, compassionate, public, and a recluse all in one! He was and still is a leader like this world has never seen before.

So, if you want people to follow you, I want to start you off with some good news. You are already halfway there! You have Jesus on your side of the ring and with that knowledge, you are ready to rise up and become a model for others to follow.

There are many self-help books out in the world that you can get. There are many practical principles that you can get from them. However, just becoming any kind of leader is not good enough. What you want to become is the kind of leader people follow because they want to, not because they have to!

## A Good Few Years Later

Well, that 13-year-old at wilderness camp grew up and as I went into ministry, I figured that I had learned a thing or two about leadership. In 1998 my husband Craig and I joined my dad and together with him and my stepmom, we built up an international ministry.

Not only did I get respect, but I started to feel really confident in my leadership. People said nice things about me and received my ministry. They did not question me, and I figured that I was well on my way to becoming the greatest example of leadership ever.

Well, if you know anything about being called to the ministry, you will learn quickly, as I did, that true ministry is not about position and recognition. My delusions of grandeur came to a dramatic halt when my dad and stepmom stepped out and handed the full care of the ministry over to us.

## A Reality Check

I thought to myself, "How hard could it be? I will just carry on doing what I always did before." Boy was I in for a rude awakening.

The first thing I discovered is that being a leader under someone and standing on your own are two very different things. Perhaps this is where you are right now.

Perhaps you have been given the chance to take on a leadership position in your church, ministry, or job. For now, things look rosy. You look at the work your superior does, and it does not seem so hard to you.

You are much like Peter who looked at how Jesus did things and figured he was enough of a leader to even give Jesus a piece of his mind and correct him for talking about going to the cross. Well, how did this loud and proud leader fare as Jesus was taken away at the Garden of Gethsemane?

It is easy to be bold when you have another leader covering you. It is not so easy when that leader is no longer there. Peter did not even make it through the night before falling flat on his face. Humiliated and ashamed, he gave up the whole idea of leading anyone and with his tail between his legs, he was off to fishing once again.

Well, I figure that Peter had it easier than I did. At least he had fishing to go back to. I did not have fishing. All I knew was the work of the ministry. We had labored together for 14 years and as this adolescent ministry was put into our lap, for the first time, I started to feel how truly heavy it was.

Having worked under my father for so long, I expected the respect from others that he had gotten. Another reality check! Respect is earned and it is not automatic. Just because I was as bold as Peter, did not mean that I was immediately ready for the full load of leadership.

## Your First Lesson: What a Leader You Are Not

And so, the first lesson you learn the moment you step out to become a leader is the same lesson I learned. That lesson is: What a leader you are *not*!

Follow me closely here, because if you allow yourself to stumble and fall on this first point, you will never make it to the end. It is reassuring to know though that you are not the only fool who has fallen on your face. You see, if you still think that you have it together and that everyone should be following you "just because" then you are not even ready for the first lesson.

If you still have your long list of excuses as to why others are chosen over you, and why no one wants to listen to you, you are not ready to begin this journey with me.

Until you get this simple, but powerful conviction, I have nothing more to share with you.

## The Big Question

So, here is a question that you have likely asked yourself and the Lord a hundred times.

>**Question:** Why doesn't anyone want to follow me?

>**Answer:** Because you are not a leader. The person you are right now is simply not good enough.

I know that is a hard reality to face, but until you do, there is no saving you. Until you realize that the reason people do not follow you, is *you*, there is no help.

You cannot change the world, but you can change yourself and so that is our starting and ending point. It is in fact the foundation of this entire teaching.

The Lord Jesus spent a full three years with Peter. He was training him day in and day out but even he failed, so do not be so hard on yourself. You will come to realize that failing is very much a part of the process of rising up.

It did not take Peter long though and before you knew it, he was once again standing before the masses with boldness, leading thousands to the Lord. There is one big difference though between Peter the hotshot in front of the other disciples, and the Peter we see before those crowds on the day of Pentecost.

## A Significant Difference

The difference lies in the fact that he was now empowered by the Holy Spirit. Together with the practical training Jesus gave him and the power the Holy Spirit imparted to him, he birthed a movement that is still resonating through the entire world today.

So, how about it? Would you like to start a movement? In a hundred years from now, wouldn't it be something to see what you started still going strong?

Well, if the Lord Jesus could transform a loud-mouthed fisherman, he can surely transform you.

Right here and now, He can make you into the kind of person people want to follow. However, just like Peter had to go on a journey, so do you.

## Becoming the "Buck"

Although I thought my journey towards leadership began as we worked with my father and stepmother to establish the ministry, the truth of the matter is that it only began when they handed the work over to us. Do you know that English expression, "The buck stops here?"

Well, only when you are that "buck" do you really start becoming a true leader. Defining moments like these have the power to make or break us. For me, I felt like it broke me. It shattered my ideas of what I thought leadership was about.

It broke my arrogance when I saw people, who I thought were faithful, turning their backs on me. It melted my resolve when I saw that my word meant nothing unless it was spoken in a power greater than my own.

## Why I Qualify to Teach You

I can teach you today, not because of my success alone. I can teach you because of my failures that led to success. I can encourage you, because I know how it feels to do and be everything you can but still fall flat. I can motivate you, because I know how it feels to serve, love, and pour out to others, only to have those same people reject you.

I can be there for you, because through all of this, I did not stay there. The Lord transformed my life and my heart into what He wanted me to be. The Lord started to show me His face and the power of His presence in my life. The Lord revealed to me the greatest leader of all time… Jesus Christ.

He showed me how He got people to follow Him, and in turn how they would follow Him in me too.

So, what do you say about changing your life? The Lord has called you to rule and reign in this life. Like Peter, He has called you to make disciples and to lead the way to the truth.

I am not denying the vision God has given to you. I am not denying the anointing, passion, and all the other good stuff you have inside.

These things will certainly get you started towards your goal, but unfortunately, they will not take you all the way there.

## The Person You Are

When the Lord first called me to apostolic office, He gave me a dramatic picture. He gave me a dream of a clay pot being smashed. I have seen that same vision many times at different times in my life since then. When I asked Him about it, He said to me, "That pot is you. The vessel you were was good for the work I had you to do up until this point. However, I have something new for you to do now. I have a new mandate for you and for you to accomplish that mandate, I need you to become a different kind of person.

If I had to release you into the mandate I have for you as you are right now, you would fail. This is not because of my calling, but because the person you are right now could not cope with it!"

There is nothing wrong with the call of God on your life. There is nothing wrong with your vision or passion. What stands in the way, is the person you are.

As things stand right now, you need to become the kind of person people want to follow. You need to become the kind of person who can accomplish the great things that God has said He would do in your life.

For all of this to happen, you need the kind of supernatural power Jesus had. You need the kind of power that can sway the masses as well as change the heart of a Pharisee.

You need to learn how to get people to follow you and as we continue, that is exactly the goal you will reach.

**CHAPTER 02**

# Getting Your Boat Into the Water

# Chapter 02 – Getting Your Boat Into the Water

Every single one of us has a desire in some way, to have others see things our way. All of us have a dream and a vision for the future and we all hope that others around us want to share that dream and vision.

But the question is, how do you get people to follow you? You have the goal, you are excited and ambitious, but how do you get others to share that same fire?

Perhaps you are the pastor of a church and you have a vision for expansion to reach out. Perhaps you want to introduce the fivefold ministry or to reach out into the community. How do you get your congregation to follow you?

Perhaps you have started a new ministry based on a vision from the Lord. Whether your vision is to minister to women, or to lay a new foundation for the Church, how do you get others to follow you?

The truth is that without other people, your vision cannot come to pass. Nowhere in Scripture will you find any leader who brought their vision to pass on their own. It always involved several people.

So, we begin this chapter with the first point that you need to remember in getting people to follow you.

## Three Steps to Remember

We were very blessed to have some vacation time in San Diego. We took some time to walk along the coastline near the harbor.

We were treated to a view of a wide variety of beautiful sailing boats. There were some pleasure boats and some small ships. In amongst those boats was a large, old sailing ship in the docks.

I nearly walked right by it until someone pointed it out to me. With its sails neatly folded up, it swayed with the tide. When I took a closer look, I noticed how beautiful it really was. It was a typical old-style, wooden sailing boat with large, white sails.

Although it was a beautiful ship, I did not notice it at all and would have walked right past unless someone had pointed it out. Firstly, its sails were all bound up and then secondly, it was tied up to the dock. Thirdly, there was no one on board.

And so, we investigated the ship a bit more. We discovered that it was used to give tours of the harbor. Along with the advertisement we found, was a full-spread photograph of the ship at open sea.

Looking at the pictures stirred my emotions. I thought to myself, "Wow! It must be so wonderful to take a ride on that ship!" But you know, when I first saw that ship at the docks with its sails all rolled up, I nearly overlooked it.

In essence, that is a picture of you right now. It is a perfect picture of you with all of your visions, hopes, dreams, and revelations.

You have the potential for something magnificent, but until you can get your boat into the water and unfurl those sails to let the wind catch them, you are not going anywhere. If you are not going anywhere, then no one is going to follow you.

You need to begin by getting your boat into the water. So, what is the first step that you need to take? Firstly, you need to plot a course.

## 1. Where Are You Going?

You might say to me, "Well, we will go out there and evangelize the lost and expand the church."

That is great, but what is your goal there? **Where are you going and how will you know when you get there?**

Do you have a very clear picture in your mind of where you want to go and of what you want to do? What is the fire and the desire of your heart? What direction has God given you?

Has God told you clearly, "I want you to build a ministry center," or, "I want you to establish a new church"? What does the end goal look like?

How can you expect people to follow you when you do not even know where you are going? You think, "Well I am the leader of this church or this ministry, people should just follow me."

Well, unless you are heading towards a goal, what do they have to follow? Will you be like the children of Israel wandering around the mountain in the desert again and again, not knowing where they were headed?

The reason they left Egypt was because they knew they were going to the Promised Land, filled with milk and honey. Had Moses not come with that goal, do you really think they would have followed him?

Can you imagine Moses saying, "Come on guys, I want you to hop on board! What we will do is make Pharaoh as angry as possible with you so that he will whip you and make you work double shifts.

After that I think we will wander around the desert for a bit and see where the wind takes us. I have heard that there is a mountain out there somewhere and perhaps we can check it out along the way...

So, what do you say, guys? Want to follow me?"

... And you wonder why no one is following you! They won't follow you if you do not know where you are going yourself.

You see, Moses came along and offered a carrot on the end of the stick. He said to them, "Alright everyone, I have got a land flowing with milk and honey. I am offering you freedom! You will eat grapes off vines that you never planted, and you will live in houses you never built."

The children of Israel needed no further motivation.

"Now you are talking! That sounds pretty good to me. Come on! Let's follow Moses!"

Of course, they did not know that they would end up taking an extended tour around that mountain.

The point is, you need a picture of where you are going and some hope to give the people. I am assuming that you got that direction from God.

## 2. What to Do When You Get There

Now that you have a picture of where you are going, what will you do when you get there?

The whole idea of going to the Promised Land was to establish Israel. Their main goal was not to sit around to drink milk and eat grapes all day... Although, I am sure that sounded like a very good idea at the time.

What are your hopes for the future? What will you make this vision into? I want to challenge you on this thinking. Do you think that everyone who hears about this fantastic goal and vision of yours, will get all excited about it?

You are so full of zeal that you cannot wait to get everyone sold on the idea, but what will you do when you get there? Again, Moses had it so well laid out.

He trained up Joshua, he had the land portioned out, and he knew exactly what they would have to do. He even knew how they would have to take the land and how they would divide it amongst the tribes. He had a very clear direction.

If you do not know where you are going and do not know what to do when you get there, you cannot give everyone a place and they have no reason to follow you.

Why should they follow you? So, before you are ready to raise the anchor and hoist the sails so that you can head out into the deep, have a picture of where you are headed.

## 3. What Are Your Capabilities?

In addition to that, what are your capabilities and what are you qualified to do?

"Ok guys, we will go out and evangelize the lost!

Unfortunately, I have never won anyone to the Lord before, but that is no problem! We will just go ahead and evangelize."

Or how about, "We will establish a fivefold ministry church. Ok... I might have to browse the internet to find out what exactly the fivefold ministry is and what they do, but you know it is the latest trend, so let's just establish a fivefold ministry church. Then I can be called an apostle and look good."

Are you trained for that position? You want to conquer the world with your big vision, but are you capable of doing it? Everyone wants to be an apostle to the nations these days but what about the rest of the fivefold ministry?

"I do not know about all that stuff, but I just want to be an apostle. You know Joe, the other pastor down the road, he is an apostle now. It's just not fair that there is only one apostle on the street now and I think I need to match up."

I hate to break it to you, but before you reach apostleship, you need to have functioned in all of the fivefold ministries first.

People won't follow you. In fact, they will talk behind your back and then stab you in the back. They might smile to your face, but they won't follow you. Even worse, the next time you look, they will be at Joe's church.

You do not know where you are going. You do not know what you will do when you get there, and you are also not secure in yourself because you do not know what you are capable of.

So, before you head out, determine what your strengths are. What can you do? Do not head out just trying to copy other people. It is a façade that will be washed away after the first storm.

## Confidence Is the Secret

If you are confident while standing at the helm of the ship, then everyone else will feel secure enough to rest while you are on board.

Know your calling and destination. Know what God has given to you and be confident in that. You see, once you have dealt with yourself and have a clear picture in your mind, just by having that assurance, others will feel comfortable around you. They will gravitate to you naturally.

We have all been around insecure leaders at one time or another. Think about someone in a leadership position (in the world or in ministry), who is insecure and do not know what they are doing. Did you ever feel like following them?

No, but what you usually do is to look at someone like that and say to yourself, "I can do a better job than that!"

You think to yourself, "Where is this guy going? What on earth was he thinking when he did that? Are you kidding? I could preach better than that!"

Why? Because he is trying to do things that he is not capable of doing. Then, instead of getting people's respect, he gets their scorn. Instead of following they say to themselves, "Man, this guy is a loser!"

## Know Who You Are

So, instead of trying to puff up the skills and abilities that you think everyone wants you to have, why not work on the abilities you do have?

Look at the anointing and the calling that you do have and stand boldly in that. Then you will outshine all other leaders. Even as I share this, I feel that there are so many who feel that they do not match up.

Everyone seems to be called to be a prophet or an apostle these days… If you are called to be an evangelist, pastor, or just to care for the poor, you feel that you do not match up. You feel that you have less than the others.

Perhaps the Lord has called you to dedicate yourself to intercession for the church, but you feel that you have to be the "great big prophet" because it is what other people expect of you.

And so, you try to put on a mask and be something you are not. Then you cannot understand why people are rejecting you and pushing you aside, thinking that you are a phony.

Well, you are a phony.

You are trying to be something you are not. It is really okay to just be an intercessor. It is quite okay to just have a gift of giving or exhortation. It is perfectly alright to just have an ability to teach and instruct.

It is alright to instruct children and if that is an ability that God has given to you and the fire that is in you, then do that! Then, as you specialize in that, you will stand out as an example.

Launch your boat into the water! Hoist those sails and people will say, "Wow! That is beautiful! I want to follow that!"

Everyone is trying to be what everyone else is. Everyone is copying everyone else and trying to rise up to all of those unseen standards.

If you are trying to be someone else, realize that they are the only person who will ever have that position. The only way that you can have their position is by pushing them off it and that is not exactly the spirit of Christ.

So, stop it! Enough! Enough of, "I want to be like the apostle next door." Let's be what God has called us to be! Let's know where we are going, and let's know what we will do when we get there.

Once you get this conviction, it is time for the next phase of your journey. It is time to plan your trip!

# Chapter 03

# Planning the Journey

# Chapter 03 – Planning the Journey

To many people, planning sounds like such a bore - especially to someone who is expressive like me. Ask my husband Craig about that. He wants to plan, and I want to just run ahead to land myself directly into the ditch.

I will never forget the first real argument we had after we took over the ministry. In times past, my father had made all the final decisions.

However, now things were different and before we made any changes or did anything, we had to be in agreement. And… my goodness! Craig was stubborn! Well, that is what I thought anyway.

I was brimming with a load of new ideas for our (then newly birthed) Prophetic School. I was ready to launch, and I wanted to do it yesterday already.

There was just one small, itsy-bitsy problem though. I had not preached the lessons for the school yet. I did not care. I figured that I could "preach them on the go" and so give people a chance to enroll right now.

Craig dug in his heels. He insisted that we took a look at the work that was involved and paced ourselves before we started. He suggested that we only release a course for enrollment when we had at least half of it completed.

I was not impressed. The expressive in me was just rearing to go. I went and complained to the Lord and He surprised me and took Craig's side. He told me that there were a lot of things I still needed to learn about leadership and one of them was to think and plan things through.

Me? Think? The Lord had to be kidding. I sucked in my pride though and instead of trying to push my agenda, I listened to my husband. Being more analytical, he could help lay things out.

It turned out that together we made the perfect team. Together we could both plan and implement. Immediately I saw why I had failed so many times in the past. I thought that all that was needed to succeed was to "keep doing" until something worked.

I was unbalanced. I needed to add the skill of planning to my attack. Together, we learned that you don't only need to know where you are going, but that you also need to plan how you will get there.

So, we sat together and worked out a plan. As it turns out, the Lord had indeed given Craig wisdom because the entire training mechanism took me a full three years to complete.

I know that I could never have completed it had we not worked it out together. When I felt like giving up, Craig kept me on track with the plan.

When there were days when I was not sure what I should do or give priority to, the curriculum and goals we set gave me the direction I needed to steer through the rocky waters.

Now I look back and see a full training mechanism for the prophets that we have even adapted for live training schools.

The goal was always clear, but the planning got us there in one piece.

Planning is needed, so stop for a moment and see what you will need for the journey ahead.

If you are planning to start a ministry, you will need a couple of things. Firstly, you will need the anointing. That is certainly a good start!

You will need some ability and things such as finances. Do you want to start a ministry center? Then you will need land. In addition to that you will need the wisdom of God.

Then once it is established, you will need further anointing and the gifts of the spirit, and a couple of fivefold ministry offices would not hurt either.

What resources do you need to establish your vision? What price will you need to pay?

> *Luke 9:62* But Jesus said to him, "No one, having put his hand to the plow, and looking back, is fit for the kingdom of God."

No one builds a house without knowing what they will need to build it. Are you planning to just "head out there" and start a ministry without thinking about what you will need?

## What Resources Will You Need?

I am glad that you have a clear vision and that you burn with a strong fire. However, you need to do a bit of planning first, otherwise by the time you get there, you won't have any materials to build that vision with.

Perhaps you will be one of those who get a rich businessman to invest into your ministry. You build your church or center and it is glorious! It has everything you ever dreamed of.

A beautiful meeting hall, a place for the kids, and every other thing a ministry could need. Now you are set! Then people come for ministry and you do not know what to do with them.

You spent all of your time establishing the natural things that you did not invest any time into getting any training from the Holy Spirit. You did not take time to get the anointing that you need to rise up as the leader you need to be.

Do you think that just by establishing a building, people will follow you? Ha! I wish that was the case! It is like a guy spending all his money on a fancy car thinking that this will make all the girls fall in love with him. I am sorry, but it does not work that way. It takes a bit more than that.

You need a personality. You can even have all the anointing in the world, but if you do not have an attractive personality, people won't follow you.

## Personality? Check!

In fact, it is sad to say, that Christians would rather follow someone with a charismatic personality than someone with a true anointing. We see this all of the time. So, do you have the personality for this job?

If you have a fire to go out and preach, do you know how to preach? It might sound like a stupid question to you, but can you preach? Are you anointed to preach? Do you have what it takes?

Let's look at something else that will make that ship stand out.

## What Do You Have That Others Do Not?

Jesus was not afraid to be bold about this. Consider the situation with the woman at the well. He came to her and said, "Give me some water."

She said, "What? Are you asking me for water?"

He replied, "Listen, if you knew who I was, you would be asking me for water. Because I have something here, that you won't find anywhere else."

He was not pandering to her. He was not afraid to approach her. He did not hint, "Thanks for the water, but you know, there is another kind of water out there, if you are interested... maybe we can talk a little bit..."

No! Jesus said, "You should be asking me. I have something here you won't find anywhere else."

So, tell me, Mr. Leader, what do you have that I cannot find anywhere else? What do you have that will impress me? What quality do you have that I want to follow?

Should people follow you simply because you have a call and a vision? That alone is not good enough. Every single believer in the Church has a call and a vision.

## First Resource - Character Strengths

So, what makes you unique? What do you have to impart to me that no one else has? If you do not have anything then it is for you to learn and to gain knowledge. You need to enroll in some courses and seek God.

If you think all these abilities will just fall out of heaven and drop into your lap, please give me your name and number. I would love to know how that happened for you, because it sure did not happen that way for me.

It takes effort. What abilities do you have that others can admire in you and follow? Consider the character traits that God has given to you.

When people describe the kind of person you are, what do you hope they say?

They should say, "<Your Name Here> is such a…"

(I meant for something positive to be placed in there.)

Think of yourself. You are so: …Friendly? …Confident? What defines you?

When I think about my husband Craig who is such a people person it is easy to say, "Craig is so approachable." It is one of his outstanding qualities and if you ever meet him, you will know exactly what I mean.

What words would you like people to use to describe you? Hopefully they would use some positive attributes to describe you. The last thing you want is for people to say, "Man, he is such a… grouch! He is so… annoying!"

No, these are definitely not characteristics we are going for here. These are not traits that will get people to follow you.

What do you have in your character that is different? It is the same concept that I discussed in the previous chapter regarding ministry.

Perhaps you think that because you are soft-hearted and loving that these are not great traits. You would rather be the tough guy! You want to be the strong guy and not the nerd.

Well, it just so happens that nerds can end up quite successful in this life if they are confident and proud of who they are.

We are who we are. Sure, through ministry training and mentorship we can change. However, there are qualities that every single one of us has that make us unique. Take those traits and be proud of them.

Stand up and show them off to the world and you will be surprised at how quickly people latch onto that. People will say, "I do not have that trait or that strength. I do not have that ability."

They will be like the cannibals that you read about in story books. Cannibals believed that if they ate someone, they would gain their strengths. It is perhaps not the prettiest picture, but it is a good one. People will want to receive from you what they do not have.

## Second Resource - Spiritual Strengths

Apostles are a dime a dozen these days. It is almost embarrassing to say that I am an apostle because they say, "Oh yes, my pastor is also an apostle."

I want to say, "Please do not insult me. I am not just 'any' apostle. I stand in the authority and the power of the Holy Spirit.

I train up the fivefold ministry and set them in place. My boast is not in my apostleship, my boast is in the mandate, anointing, and ability that God has given to me.

It is in the fact that whoever He puts on my knee, I will raise up to be a warrior by putting a sword in their hand and sending them out to be victorious. Now *that's* what makes me unique."

What makes you special? "I am a prophet. I am an apostle. I am a…" Who cares? They are a dime a dozen.

What spiritual ability do you have that is unique? The Holy Spirit manifests His gifts and anointing in varied ways.

He has worked this way since the beginning of time. So, while you are running around trying to hang onto all your titles, you are missing the most important point of all. People do not follow titles. *They follow the power of God.*

## The Power Is Not in the Title

You can say what you want. You can call yourself an M.D., PhD, CEO, Apostle, or a DMin. In fact, you can call yourself anything you want to. However, when you stand up without the mantle of authority or anointing, you are no different to a balloon that's covered over with papier mâché.

It may have a good face and image but there is just a bunch of air inside. People might follow you for the first five minutes while you are looking good. Unless you stand up in boldness and in the anointing though, your little ship will be scuttled. It won't make it out into the deep sea.

So why should I follow you? Before you can even get your ship into the water, you should know the answer to that question.

## Your Checklist

So, let's bring all of our points together now and see how you fare.

1. Do you know where you are going?
2. What will it look like when you get there?
3. What do you need to build the vision?
4. What change do you need in yourself to accomplish your vision?

Once you have a clear answer for each of these questions, it will be time for you to set sail.

**CHAPTER 04**

# Time to Set Sail

# Chapter 04 – Time to Set Sail

People have a strange idea when it comes to leadership. They say to themselves, "I will wait for people to like me. I will wait for people to follow me. Once that happens, I will launch out with my vision."

I have some bad news for you. You will wait for another 50 years. In fact, you will wait until the day you die. People won't follow you until you get up to lead.

Do not think that everyone wants to jump in your ship or come alongside while you are still sitting in the dry docks. They will treat you the same way that I treated that sailing ship I saw in San Diego.

I walked past that ship, not seeing its full potential, because it looked dull and boring. No one will follow you until your sails are unfurled and you are sailing out into the deep.

## God Is Waiting for You

You see, you are waiting to become the right person. You are waiting until the time is right.

You keep waiting for God, but what you do not realize is that God is waiting for you.

Nobody will follow you, until you have the courage to press forward with the vision God has given to you.

You have to take the first step. You cannot wait forever. I love this scripture:

> **John 12:32** *And I, if I am lifted up from the earth, will draw all peoples to Myself.*

He was speaking of how He would die. However, it is also a fantastic picture of leadership. "When I am lifted up, **then** I will draw all men."

Let me tell you, there is a price to pay. It is the same price that Jesus paid. It is a walk of death to the flesh. When it comes to your natural abilities it is a walk of weakness and total submission to the Lord.

You won't draw any men unto you until you rise up and are lifted up. Do you want to get bitter because you see other leaders out there who are arrogant and dominating God's people?

They may be arrogant, proud, and in deception, but they have been lifted up and they are drawing men unto themselves. What are you doing sitting in the dry docks? You are sitting around waiting for someone to hitch a ride on your ship... but your sails are still tied up?!

## God Directs a Moving Ship

Step out! Get moving! The best part is that once your boat is in the water, God can direct it.

We often wait for God to give direction, but when you hear His voice, He says, "Get your boat in the water and once it is moving, I can direct the rudder. Only then can I give you direction."

You want the whole picture ahead of time though. You will be waiting another 20 years if that is what you want.

That is like someone who wants to be in prophetic office, but has not even enrolled in a prophetic school. They want to become a prophet but they are not willing to receive training from a mentor or the Lord.

You think, "I will just wait until something happens to me."

You want to establish a church and do not know how. So, you say, "I will just wait until I get the clear go ahead to move forward."

You will wait for a long time.

Learn what you have to learn! Do what you have to do but get yourself moving!

As you start moving, God can direct you. Take the opportunity to minister to those who are already around you. Use the opportunities that are already there. If you are in a local church, already leading a ministry or business, move forward.

Do not wait for everyone else to get "ready" before you decide to take a step forward!

Otherwise you will be like my family first thing in the morning. There we are, sitting in the car, waiting for the girls to come down and join us. We have to wait because they have to do their make-up.

If I had to let them decide when they are ready to go, we would never get moving. I am in charge here. I decide when we move! If I sat around waiting for them to get ready, we would be two hours late for every meeting rather than the usual one hour.

If you move, others will follow. You cannot wait for others to follow before you lead.

Joshua understood this principle very well. He didn't say, "Okay guys, we have to do this whole foreskin cutting thing and then we have to cross the Jordan. So, I was thinking… Monday is good for me. Is Monday good for you?

No? Wedding on Monday? Ah okay, how about Tuesday then? Yes? No? Hmm… we will have to reschedule this meeting because it is already past lunch…"

How many church meetings are like that? Lord, deliver us! No, Joshua did not ask for any opinions. He did not take a poll.

Instead he said, "This is what God said. Sorry chaps! We have a little circumcision to do today and then get ready to carry all our equipment in three days, because we will cross the Jordan into the Promised Land.

If there is anyone who does not want to come, then you can stay on the other side, but we will go!"

Strangely enough, no one argued with Joshua. Maybe it was because he had that flint knife in his hand at the time…

Set your sights, prepare yourself, and then launch.

Whether someone is following you or not is really irrelevant. If you already have your sights set with a clear focus on your goal and you step out with confidence and ability, you will be surprised.

You will turn around to find people naturally following you. I am not saying that you won't feel insecure. I am not saying that your legs won't be shaking.

I know that on the inside you are saying, "Oh Lord please, let me not mess up! Please Lord, don't let me hit that wall."

Sure, we all have fears and insecurities. However, unless you step out and try how will you find out what you are capable of?

If you think that you can just sit in your comfy lounge and then suddenly "BAM" you have become a leader, you have the wrong idea!

Nobody ever became a leader that way. It happens as the journey progresses. Even Moses was no great leader yet when God first appeared to him. In fact, he was a wimp!

Look at Gideon! What a loser he was! He even fleeced the Lord a few times. "What a great man of God." No, he was not a great man of God when he started out.

Look at Solomon! He was but a child when he started out. However, as each of their journeys progressed, look at what happened to them!

They made choices others did not. They did things others were not prepared to do. That is what awaits you in the next phase of your journey. We will focus on that in the next chapter.

## Summary of Chapters 1-3

Write down and apply these three simple points:

1. Know where you are going.
2. Get what you need to accomplish your vision when you get there.
3. Step out and launch that vision.

## CHAPTER 05

# How to Get People to Admire You

# Chapter 05 – How to Get People to Admire You

My daughters had caught onto a new soft toy craze called "Webkins". They were cute soft toys that each had a tag and printed code which then allowed them to go online and join a virtual world.

They, especially my youngest daughter Rebekah, thought this was the coolest thing in the whole world. She just loved these things. She had ducks, swans, dogs, cats, and even some creatures I could not identify!

She had a whole menagerie in her bedroom. It was to the point where although I was sure there had been a floor once upon a time, it had now been transformed into a Webkins gallery.

Any money she managed to charm out of grandpa, or received for pocket money, was invested into the next and best Webkins release.

Well, not satisfied to simply overcrowd her bedroom, she had come up with an idea for the ultimate Webkins experience. She was going to host the best teddy bear show ever. She started sneaking boxes into the house from the garage to form little mountains.

As I walked into my lounge unsuspectingly one evening, a big surprise awaited me. I discovered a complete setup of boxes and blankets there.

She had all the toys categorized. Then the nagging began. "Mommy please, come! I am going to do a teddy bear show! Please come watch."

She kept on nagging even when I was in the middle of something.

And so, I thought, "Let me give her five minutes."

I sat down and had to endure the teddy bear show. As it turned out, it was not a five minute teddy bear show. It was not even a ten minute show. Rebekah is a raging expressive and so it was a long… long teddy bear show!

At the end of that long show, Rebekah asked, "Mommy, what did you think?"

What Mommy thought was the most important thing to her. She was thrilled to hear me say, "That was fantastic! You did a great job."

You see, there is a child in each one of us who is asking the same question. That child wants to hang upside down on the bars at the playground and exclaim, "Mommy! Look at me! What do you think?"

There is a need for recognition in each one of us. As a child it is alright to put on shows motivated by this need, and to then expect Mommy to meet it by saying,

"You are so clever! You are so creative! That is the best show I have ever seen."

However, as we grow up, we realize that these shows are not always acceptable. We realize that performing to meet the needs inside of us have the potential to drive us beyond what God intended.

Throughout the last few chapters, I have been emphasizing the importance of knowing who you are, and of standing up in what God has given to you.

The big question is though, how do you overcome this battle? How do you shine with what is inside of you without allowing those needs to dominate you?

## Why People Should Admire You

If you are still working on getting your needs met correctly, what is the point of having others admire you? Well, if people do not admire you, they also won't follow you.

Jesus told us to make disciples of all nations. Do you know what that means? It means that you have to be the mentor. You need to be the leader.

So, why would someone want to follow you? They will want to follow you because they admire something in you that they don't have. So, the question is, "How do you get people to admire you?"

How do you get them to see that "something" inside of you? How do you get them to drop everything and follow you instead of somebody else? Well, that is the purpose of this chapter.

## What *Not* to Do

I will quickly go over the "what *not* to do" section of this chapter. I do not like to emphasize the negative, so I will go over it quickly so that we can move onto the good stuff.

## Do Not Push People to Follow You

I have four kids. There is a phrase I will hear repeatedly throughout the day from at least one of them. It goes like this, "Stop bossing me around! Mommy! Deborah is telling me what to do again!"

Then Deborah shouts, "Mom, Jessica is telling me what to do again!"

You know how it is with kids. Well, this does not just happen with kids, it happens with adults too. We all grew up with the "bossy boots" in class. There was always "that" kid who pushed you to do what they wanted you to do.

If you look back though, you see that the kid just had a desperate need for recognition. They wanted you to notice that they were a "big shot" so badly. They were like the little child on the playground shouting, "Look at me, Mom! Look at how wonderful I am."

However, on the receiving end, how did you respond to them pushing you around? I am sure that you did not take it well at all. You did not like people like that.

You did not like people that forced you to like things that they liked.

When I look in the Scriptures, I see the perfect example of this in King Saul. Along comes David, who won a huge victory for Saul. He slayed Goliath and his ten thousand. However, Saul was not impressed with David at all, was he?

He became jealous of David and then tried to push his own agenda. He tried to push himself forward. He gathered all the strong and mighty so that he could say, "Look at how great I am, guys!"

What is the greatest sin that David committed as far as Saul was concerned? It was that the people loved David more than they loved him. The people recognized David's abilities.

Instead of being part of the people and encouraging David so he would be known as the good guy, he did the complete opposite. He tried to push David down and force himself to the front. He made the same mistake with Samuel and the sacrifice.

He pushed his own agenda. When God gave him a direct order, instead of obeying God, he pushed his own agenda. And so, today Saul is not known as the most loved king in Israel. To this day when someone mentions Saul, King of Israel, everyone says, "Oh yes! That was the guy who messed it up badly!"

Why? It was because he pushed his own way. He was nothing more than a big old "bossy boots" and no one likes them in this world.

What are you like when you attend a meeting or get a chance to minister? Are you pushing your own view and agenda? Are you telling everyone to listen to you as you share your latest revelation?

Then you cannot understand why people are trying to find the door… Nobody wants to be forced into anything, or attacked with your vision.

## What to Do

The key instead is to look outward. It is not what they think of you that matters. What you think of them though, makes all the difference in the world.

If you want people to admire you, then stop trying to make them admire you. Start admiring things in them and they will naturally start to admire you.

### Admire the Potential in Others

When you see the hope in others, then you become the answer to their need. You become the source.

You mistakenly think that in order for people to admire you, your whole big list of qualities and your grand vision are required. You think that you must explain your vision to them along with how fantastic you are.

You think that at the end they will respond with, "Wow! What a great man of God." Forget it! They are looking for the door. They are bored. They do not care.

Rather sit them down and identify what God has given to them and what their potential is. Help them identify their ministry and see what you can help them with.

When they realize that you have what they need, you will get their admiration right away. You will gain it not because of what you could do, but because of what you admired in *them*.

However, when you are insecure in yourself, you tend to become too introspective and therefore try to push your own agenda. When you do this, you do not see the real potential in others.

Let's be honest with one another. You want others to admire you and see your potential, don't you? Well, do you think that the rest of the world is any different to you?

They need it just as much! If you fulfill that need and have faith, love, and hope for them, then people will admire you all the time.

Who is admired in this world? Having experienced many different cultures, I know that there are a lot of clever people out there. There are a lot of talented and skilled people in the world.

Whether in the field of computers or the arts, there are so many people who are gifted. There are so many preachers in the Church who can preach well. What sets you apart?

For people to admire you, there has be a spark or something inside of you that is different from others.

## Be Attainable

I can sum it up in one point. The key to the "something" inside of you is that it should be attainable. Not only is it important that you see the potential in others, but whatever it is that God has given to you, needs to be attainable to others.

Be honest with how you view others. You get this super-duper hotshot who gets big words from God but seems so far above you. You think it is great, but you realize that you will never attain to that.

What kind of hope does that give you? You might go to one or two of their conferences to see what a hotshot they are, but you won't give your life for a person like that. You won't give your heart and follow them to the ends of the earth. You won't be like David's mighty men who laid down their lives for him.

So, these hotshots are some lonely people. They have a great vision but they are so far beyond anything anyone can attain to. Then when they fall, they fall alone.

Do you really want to be a leader like that? Do you want a position where everyone hero worships you, or do you want to change lives for God?

If you really want to change lives, then you need to come down a bit and give the people under you some hope. Here is a good example:

> **John 14:12** *Most assuredly, I say to you, he who believes in Me, the works that I do he will do also; and greater works than these he will do, because I go to My Father.*

Here is the most perfect man who ever lived. He raised the dead and healed the sick. He did the impossible, However, He didn't say, "The works that I do… forget it, suckers! No one can ever touch me. I am the Messiah, and no one will ever be able to move like I move! You just stand right there and worship me!"

So why is it that we worship Jesus? We love Him because He first loved us. We worship Him because He gave us everything right to the very last drop of His blood!

We adore Him because He said, "Everything that I have, I am giving to you. I raised the dead, but you will do greater works. I am not content for you to do only what I did, but I want you to rise up higher."

With this kind of love, you want to give your life for Him, and His disciples literally did. When the Pharisees stood up with their big speeches and long robes, which one of them was willing to die for the other?

No, instead they fought amongst themselves and vied for the top positions. When they fell though, they fell alone. In contrast, consider how many of the early church Christians gladly sacrificed their lives for the Lord.

Peter said that they gave up their homes and families. Why did they do this? What made Jesus so different? It is because He said, "The things that I have, the things that you admire in me, if you stick with me, you will get it all."

Jesus had the ability to sway the crowds, to teach, and heal the sick and He offered all of this to His disciples. If you want to be admired, then start saying things like that.

You should be saying, "Do you see these things that God has given to me? These things are not just for me. I have this for one reason only and it is to give it to you."

## Giving Hope

I dare say that it is what sets our fivefold ministry training apart. We didn't learn all of the principles just so that we could boast about our great knowledge on the fivefold ministry. No, the intention has always been to learn and go through the training so that others could enter into the fruit of our labor, just as Apostle Paul said.

God raised me up so that I can look at someone with a prophetic call and intend to raise them up to become a better prophet than I can be. In fact, that is the point of all this training!

Are you telling this to those who are following you, or are you too afraid that they will rise up to your position and look better than you? You need to give them a hope that they can attain.

There are some you will mentor and some you will train who will rise up and become better than you. Well, I should hope so, because otherwise you did not do your job very well.

However, keep in mind that you are the originator. It does not matter how high they go, how much more they learn, or if their skill increases a hundred-fold. Jesus said we would do greater things. Peter stood up on the Day of Pentecost and converted a couple of thousand people in one day.

Peter's shadow healed the sick. He did indeed rise up as Jesus promised. Did Jesus ever step in and try to put Peter "back in his place?" He did not need to, because Peter knew where he got that power from!

Peter knew the price he had to pay to walk in that power. And so, no matter how high those under you rise up, if you have the attitude of giving them hope, they will always see you above them.

Even though you realize that they surpassed you quite some time ago, they will always see you over them. Why is this? It is because you are the originator and you are the one who started them on their road.

It is just like my daughter Rebekah who needs me to notice her. No matter how old she gets, or how much she matures, I will always be her mother. Our relationship will change, but there will always be a part of her that will respect me and value my opinion.

Why? It is because I always gave her that vote of confidence. I have experienced this even in my own life. There are times when you rise up in things and surpass your spiritual parents, but you still seek their approval. It is because they started you on your road and you respect them for that.

## Getting Rid of the Fear

Unfortunately, there is a great fear in the body of Christ. It says, "If people rise up higher than me, then what will happen to me? I will become yesterday's news."

Why don't you take the chance and take the risk for a change? Try it out! If they do not have hope in you that they can rise up and receive what you have, then they will go somewhere else.

You can follow an empty leader for just so long, like the children of Israel followed Saul, before you realize that this leader won't take you where you want to go. You realize that this leader is only trying to fulfill their own vision and that they are just using you.

We both know these kinds of leaders. You do not want to be one of them. However, you will become like them if you do not stop for a moment and look at the potential in others. Give them hope!

It's like that when I identify a ministry calling in someone and then tell them that I have what they need to attain that calling. I also tell them that everything I have is available to them and that I am ready to impart it to them.

As a result, people follow. It is because they have hope. I do not need to lord anything over them and keep telling them that they must obey because "God said so!"

You can demand only so much before people have enough of you. It just takes someone else to come along and they will run for that person in an instant. It is because that person gives them a glimmer of hope.

Then when that person lets them down, they continue to look until they find the kind of leader we are talking about here… A *Jesus* kind of leader.

## Offer These Three Encouragements:

1. I see the potential inside of you.
2. I have what you need to fulfill that potential.
3. I am prepared to take you there.

You want to follow a leader like that, so why don't you become a leader like that?

**CHAPTER 06**

# Getting People to Follow 101

# Chapter 06 – Getting People to Follow 101

I look at David and his mighty men. Have you ever taken the time to notice the qualities these guys had?

One of them killed a couple of hundred Philistines alone on a snowy day. We are talking about hand to hand combat here. Can you even imagine it?

Some of these mighty men were quite incredible. They killed more than David did. They also did greater things than David did. They were probably even taller or more good looking.

You do not see them trying to rise up and push David out of the way though. On the other hand, you do not see David pushing them down either. He took his mighty men everywhere with him. He entrusted his life into their hands.

They lived together and did everything together. He had such a respect for them that they are listed in scripture. Here is a leader who was not afraid to have people who were stronger than him under his command.

Also, those big, strong men didn't say, "Come on David, get out of the way. We can fight this battle better than you!"

No, because *it was not his skill that counted, but his ability to lead.*

# 1. You Do Not Need to Know Everything

I would hope that God would bring you people who have skills and abilities that you do not have. It is not about knowing everything or even about being the best at everything. It is about being able to lead and giving people hope and direction.

## Recognizing the Position of Others

I look at the scripture where Nicodemus came to Jesus at night. They debate a bit of doctrine and it says:

> **John 3:10** *Jesus answered and said to him, "Are you the teacher of Israel, and do not know these things?*

I know that Jesus was challenging him here, but do you notice that Jesus recognized this man's position? He clearly recognized that he was a master in Israel.

He did not question him by saying, "I suppose you think you are a master in Israel, but let me teach you a few things..."

Jesus wanted to convince Nicodemus to see things his way. He wanted to change this man's entire doctrinal viewpoint. He did not do it by correcting the poor guy and saying, "You bunch of Pharisees! You think you have all the answers, but you do not. You are stupid!"

Instead, Jesus recognized his position and then went on to share things that Nicodemus did not know. Jesus did not push the man down, but rather gave him the respect and admiration that Nicodemus likely needed.

As a result, he became a follower. Are you doing that with others around you? You see someone who has a lot of potential and is rising up. Perhaps they are a bit overzealous, but are you feeling threatened? What are you going to do?

## A Leader Rallies Other People

Will you push them down? You could say, "Yes, I see that you are a master at what you do!" Will you recognize that in them? People think that to be a great leader you must have all the skills and abilities needed to fulfill your vision.

And yes, it is good to have some skill, but that is not what makes a good leader.

There are millions of people in the world who are professionals, highly educated and capable. Does this make them good leaders? Not at all. A leader is someone who can rally people around them who do have those skills and then give them direction and hope.

This is what God is calling you to do. What do you end up doing instead though? You go around touting your own abilities saying, "Look at me, Mom! I have a degree in this and that! This is *my* revelation! This is *my* vision."

You think that everybody will drop everything and follow you, just because you are so capable. You have never been more wrong in your life!

*People will not follow you because you are capable. People will follow you, because you see the capabilities in them.*

If you want to deal with the need for recognition in your own life, start giving recognition to others.

If you want people to admire you, then start admiring others.

That characteristic alone will be admirable. It will be more than what you find in 90% of the leaders in the Church. Who is really paying the price?

No one is saying, "I see the potential in you!" Instead they are saying, "Hey guys, look at my great new business plan! We will expand this church. We will get a new building. I have a great big vision!"

You sit at the back of the meeting thinking to yourself, "What exactly does that man's vision have to do with me?"

## Nobody Wants to Be the Underdog

Nobody likes to be the underdog or to feel that they are stupid, even if they are! So, if you make people feel stupid and insecure, will this make you feel like a great leader?

Raise people up who are under you and it immediately elevates you higher. You can be a leader no matter how insecure you are and even if you were born on the wrong side of town. It does not matter how many mistakes you have made, or how many people have left you. You can become a leader right now.

Leaders are not born. God can make you into something. However, it will require some change. You won't wake up one morning to discover that you have become a leader overnight.

There will be some challenges. The first thing you will learn is what a leader you are not. You will face some deaths and struggles along the way, but you can rise up and get people to admire you.

This week, why not give it a try and begin to recognize the ability in others? Be it at work or at church, give it a try.

I am not talking about just giving compliments. I am talking about recognizing people's abilities and strengths.

Learn to say words such as, "I admire in you…"

How many times have you said that this week?

"I truly admire how you…"

"You really have an ability to…"

"You are so much better than me at…"

Do you think that you will be putting yourself down if you say those things? Quite the contrary is true.

Giving recognition puts you in a position of superiority and of leadership. You give them an opportunity to lool up to you, by being loving and not doing it in an arrogant way.

People won't take advantage of you but will admire you more.

Learn to see the hopes, dreams, and goals in others and then become the solution to those things. Then you will find that people naturally admire you and want to go anywhere you want to go.

## 2. You Do Not Need to Do Everything

When we started our original online Prophetic School in 1999 things got busy really fast. While my father did most of the teaching, I was taking care of the students and their projects.

After some time, I was handed all of the schools to run by myself. With a couple of lecturers in place to help me, I went on doing what I had always done.

This time though I had more work than before, but it did not deter me. I just kept on working all day and all night long.

It did not take long for me to hit a wall of exhaustion. I was running around like a headless chicken, trying to make it all work. I had forgotten something profound. I was not alone.

It took a while for the Lord to get through to me with the most incredible revelation.

That revelation was: I did not need to do everything by myself! It was a rhema word sent right from the throne room of God.

## The One-Man Show Must Go

Because I was responsible for the training side of the ministry, I figured that I had to do all of the work as well. I had written most of the training and of course I was the only one who knew how to handle the students.

Well, that is what I thought anyway. That thinking nearly killed me though. I was overwhelmed, not because the work was too much, but because I figured that if I wanted the job done right I had to do it all by myself.

The Lord had given me a fantastic group of lecturers to work with. Clearly it was time to do some delegating.

Do you know what the worst consequence of making this mistake is? It is not that you work yourself to the point of falling into bed completely exhausted every night.

The worst is that it tells everyone around you that they are not good enough for the job. Could you imagine if Jesus had this kind of attitude? The New Testament Church would never have been birthed.

While He still walked the earth, He sent His disciples out two by two so that they could reach further than He could alone. Apostles Peter and Paul continued in this pattern, by sending others ahead of them when they traveled.

It was not uncommon for Paul to send Timothy, Titus, or Silas ahead of him before he reached a region. Then he would often also leave them behind to finish the work.

As a result, the early church grew rapidly. What is the real problem here? I would have to say that the real problem is fear and pride.

Thoughts start coming to your mind, "What if the people like this other person more than me? What if more people follow them than me?"

Well, if you have that kind of fear, then you are not a real leader, are you? People will not follow you just because you can do the job by yourself, but because you are leading the way to a destination.

Just because you are not the one doing all of the ministry, work, and organization does not mean that you are no longer leading. Quite the opposite is true!

Was Jesus afraid to send His disciples out? Can you imagine Him wringing His hands saying, "What happens if I give them this power and then people admire them more than me?"

Thank goodness that He did not have this attitude. Not only did He give them all He had, but He backed them as well. What was the result? The result was that each time one of His disciples ministered, it was His name they mentioned. They did not take the glory for themselves.

Why was that? It was because they knew where the power came from. It is the same with the people that you work with as well.

Do not be afraid to give them a vote of confidence and let them do the work that you cannot do. Also do not be afraid to give them a chance to do the work that you can do.

## The Common Goal

When you think in this way, you give everyone a common goal to work towards. There is just something about us humans that loves to be part of a cause.

The early church was part of a magnificent cause to win the world for Jesus. Paul and his team had a cause to reach the Gentiles. Gideon had a cause and so did Moses.

As a result, the people gathered around. Why do you think the mighty men hung around David?

Firstly, because he knew what he was doing and how he was going to get there, but above all, he gave them a part in his cause.

It was their cause and not only his own. Do you want people to follow you to the ends of the earth? Then it is time that you start saying things such as:

- Our ministry
- Our vision
- The work we are doing

Dump the solo act and make the people around you a part of what God is doing in your life. Let them feel that they have an important part to play.

As the ministry grew, we started reaching out more into social networks and as feedback started coming in, I noticed a trend. People were not writing in and saying, "Apostle Colette Toach is the best!"

Instead they said, "A.M.I. has done so much for me," or, "Everyone in this ministry is such an important part of my life."

It made me realize that we were not a one-man show. We were a ministry. We were a body. We were a team. It was now God's work and it was all about *we* and not about *I*.

## Hand Out Some "Heart Shares"

Something incredible happens when people following you have a place. The ministry vision becomes their baby as much as yours.

When finances come in, they feel as if they played a part in bringing them in. When there is a loss or an obstacle they no longer think, "This is the pastor's problem, not mine." No, instead they say, "We have this problem. What can I do?"

If you want people to care about your vision and ministry as much as you do, then you need to give them some "heart shares" in it. You need them to own that vision in their heart.

When a company wants to go public and expand, they sell shares on the market. Well, we do not approve of that kind of "market share" in the Kingdom of God. Rather we trade in "heart shares" where each person belongs to the work God is doing and that work belongs to them.

They must feel as if they are a vital part of this vision of yours and if they do, they will care for it as their own.

No one will love another person's child as much as they love their own! So why not let down your guard and say, *we* instead of *I* all of the time?

Then step back and allow each one a chance to participate. Assess the abilities of those who are following you and give them a chance to step to the fore.

How often do you see this in the Church today? Not too often I am afraid. How ready is the "Senior Pastor" to hand his pulpit over? There is that familiar fear, isn't there? "What if people like the other guy's preaching more than mine?"

It is only an insecure leader who thinks like that and we will be dealing with more of this a little bit later.

## *My Own Experience*

For the longest time I was the one who wrote a lot of the announcements for all of our new materials or teachings. (Yes, I really did learn to do everything first before handing it over.)

I was stuck with it for quite some time, because I was the person who seemed to be the best at it. Then the Lord started adding to our team and I discovered that there was someone else who could write even better than I could.

You cannot imagine my relief! Once I recognized her ability, I put her to work and helped her to refine her writing. Before long, people were responding to her letters and encouragements just like they had done to mine.

Do you know what a powerful impact it had on the ministry? Not only were people receiving fresh encouragement, but I now had time to put into other projects (...like writing this book for example).

I won't lie! There was a little twinge of regret to hand over the little baby I had carried for a while. I will never look back though, because by stepping back, my time and ability to do God's work doubled.

The same thing happened to me in the ministry arena. Craig and I were always the ones to step forward and provide counsel and ministry to everyone who knocked on our door. Eventually though with us starting our first ministry center in San Diego, things got so busy we could not cope.

It was almost like the Lord was twisting our arms. You see, I had been faithful to hand over certain tasks to my team, such as letter writing and the training online. However, the Lord wanted me to hand over more.

It happened really out of necessity. Someone visited the center for a season of ministry and Craig and I could just not get there. So, the resident couple at that time, Ronald and Denise Jordan, had to step in and do the job.

What do you know... they could minister! Sure, I had given them a chance to minister with us as a team, but this was their first solo flight.

Not only could they minister, but they exceled in it. By the time we did make it up there, they had laid such a foundation, that all Craig and I had to do, was finish up. I thought to myself, "Why didn't we do this before?"

Ron and Denise had spent days teaching, encouraging, and preparing that person. Is this not what Silas and Timothy did for Paul? They went ahead and got the people ready for the message that was coming. As a result, they became a team that was unshakable.

I tell you what though, after that time, Ron and Denise were stronger than ever. They stuck to us more and when tough times came, they were the first to commit and follow through.

They were not just employees or staff. This was now their ministry and because they were a part of it, they continued to give everything to it.

Where do you stand right now? What responsibilities are you handing out to those around you that are capable? Are you trying to do everything by yourself?

Give it a rest! If you want people to follow you, give them something to invest their hearts into.

Give them some "heart shares" in your vision and watch as they stick to you like glue.

## 3. You Need to Keep Your Finger on the Pulse

So, you do not need to know everything, and you do not need to do everything. So, pack your bags, book your flight to Hawaii and let the vacation begin.

I do not think so. Just because you do not need to do all the work yourself, does not mean your job got any easier.

Again, this was a lesson I learned when I took over the training of the prophets. I decided, "Okay! I am going to delegate some of my jobs to the lecturers!" So, I gave them tasks and responsibilities and stepped back, quite chuffed that I was making progress as a leader.

A few weeks into it though and I felt like everything came crashing down. I did what God had said. I had trained them and handed the jobs over. Why then was no one doing their jobs?

I did not want to walk around acting like a sergeant major, but I was getting more than a little stressed at how disorganized things suddenly were.

I was complaining when my dad came once again with that perfect word of advice at the right time. He asked me some simple questions:

"Did you make it clear what you wanted to be done?"

"Did you give them a deadline to do it in?"

"Did you tell them what you wanted them to do once they were finished?"

Good questions! I just assumed that because I knew how to do the job that they would too. I assumed that because I knew how to mark projects and follow up students, they would just copy me and do it also.

## Assume Nothing

It was right then that my dad gave me two words to live by regarding leadership. He said to me, "Colette, assume nothing!"

You see, there is a reason we have 66 books in the bible that cover every kind of topic you can think of. There is a reason that the Lord went into so much detail from Leviticus to Deuteronomy.

Did you ever wonder why these books are so long-winded? The Lord left nothing to chance. He covered all His bases and assumed nothing. Instead He gave the Israelites a very clear track to run on.

Are you doing that for the people who are following you? If you have asked someone to do a job for you, do not think, "Whew! I am glad that is over with. Now I can go and take a break and forget about it."

You wish! No, just because you are not doing the job, does not mean you don't have to remember everything about it.

After that, I took some of my father's advice, and what do you know… there was an instant turn around. I started to make things clearer.

Not only did I tell them exactly what job I wanted them to do, but I also let them know how much time they had to do it in.

It gave everyone security. Take note of this lesson, because it is one that you will live again and again. In fact, if anyone lets you down, I bet it is because you did not follow those three little points.

1. Lay out the responsibility in detail along with what is expected.
2. Give a deadline.
3. Tell them what to do when they are done.

Was Jesus any different? He told His disciples exactly what to do. He put them into teams of two and told them not to take a coat with them. He told them how to handle the people and to be as gentle as doves, but as wise as serpents.

Once they were done, they all returned to Jesus and we see how he instructs them on their lack of faith and how to deal with problems they could not face correctly (such as when they couldn't cast out the demon from the child).

## Structuring is Key

I know that there are a lot of us who do not like structure and planning a lot, but it really is essential. This was another mistake I faced when we had our first ministry center in San Diego.

While our resident team lived there, we lived elsewhere. So, it was really important that they communicated with us about all the needs at the center. Silly things like bills, appointments, and things that needed fixing.

It was around this time, that I thought for sure my usually amiable husband was going to blow his lid. We would arrive to stay for a weekend and the problems would begin.

He would discover that things were broken and in need of repairs. Bills were unpaid and services were about to be suspended. Instead of spending the time in ministry like we should have, it became a time of "catch up" where we ran around putting out fires.

The bottom line here? We needed a bit of order and structure. We made the mistake of thinking that everyone there would just take notice and that they would all jump in and help.

The problem is, because we did not structure it properly, everyone thought that everyone else had taken care of it. Does this sound familiar to you?

Think about the last supper and how Jesus organized that. He grabbed a few of His disciples and He did not only tell them where they were to have it, but also how to secure the room.

Jesus did not run off and do all of the work, but He organized it. He remembered that there needed to be a feast and He organized the plans. He had His finger on the pulse of everything.

He did not need to do the work, but He gave clear instructions to the people who needed to do the job. As a result, the dinner went off without a hitch.

Well, that is if you discount the little betrayal act by Judas during the second course…

## Be in the Know

So, when we arrived at our center and everything was in chaos, whose fault was it? The flesh in me wanted to blame everyone, but in the end, we found that finger pointing at ourselves.

We made the mistake of thinking that just because we had handed the actual work over, that we had handed the full responsibility over as well.

No, as a leader you will always need to have your finger on the pulse of what is happening. This is the load of responsibility that Apostle Paul spoke of when he spoke about the weight of the churches.

It was not the work that weighed him down. It was not the teaching or the preaching. What weighed him down was the spiritual load of care.

This is what sets one leader apart from another and it is the true price of leadership. Only when you have been there will you understand it.

I can imagine that Apostle Paul lay in bed at night and wondered how the churches were doing. I am sure that he would have wondered if their needs were met and if they were following after the Lord.

I bet he wondered if they received his teaching and if they were rising up in the Lord, or if they were being swayed by the persecution they were facing.

I know this, because these are some of the things that cross my mind when I lie in bed at night. I am thinking about all the emotional, spiritual, and natural needs of everyone who is with us.

I realize that it is not just my life that is influenced by our decisions, but many others as well.

This is the true load that you will always carry, so be sure that you carry it well. This is why you cannot push yourself to try and know everything, or do everything at all times.

Rather dedicate your time to carrying the care of responsibility and being there for your team, than feeling you need to be the one-man show.

# CHAPTER 07

# Keeping Those That Follow

# Chapter 07 – Keeping Those That Follow

Ruby, my youngest daughter, was just not being herself. She woke up grumpy every day and was snapping at her sisters. It was another crazy time in our lives.

I had just given birth to Michael, my youngest and final child. In amongst that, Craig and I were trying to figure out how to handle the load of A.M.I. that we had just been given. Somewhere in between all that, I was also trying to fight off the baby blues and the odd pity party about never seeing my figure again.

In light of the situation, I was long overdue for a pity party. Who could blame me, right? In a moment like this, I could have easily justified myself with a little "me time."

However, if you are a parent, you gave up the rights to any "me time" the moment the sperm met the egg. Well, the same holds true for the realm of the spirit and spiritual leadership as well.

My daughter was certainly not being herself and so I pulled her aside to talk. She was having her own personal crisis. She was afraid that because a new baby was here, that she would not be my "little Ruby" any longer.

It only took a few cuddles and kisses to take her fears away and to tell her that I still cared. She did not need much, but for that little moment she just needed to feel special.

All of us have days like this and if you are a leader, then it is for you to watch for the signs in those around you. Learn to notice when they have days like this.

## 4. Keep Watch

It is just so easy to get swept away with all the things you need to remember. You get so busy keeping your finger on the pulse of everything that you forget to look up into the faces of those around you.

Could you imagine a doctor like that? Imagine a doctor walking into a room, without greeting you he just proceeds to taking your pulse and monitoring your vital signs.

He might be a good medic, but his bedside manner could leave him without patients in a very short space of time. Watch that you do not become a leader like that!

You can get so busy with all the needs and cares that you can forget that the greatest care is how the people around you feel and how they are doing.

# The Skill of Other Orientation

I know that when there is a job to do, it is easy to overlook it if someone is having a bad day. That is why learning the skill of other orientation is so important.

If you want people to follow you, then you need to watch for the signs and notice how they are doing. This is a habit that you can develop over time.

Again, Jesus was a master at this. In fact, He was so good that He could sense a person's spirit as well. When Nathanael came to him, He said, "Ah, a man in whom there is no guile." Nathanael answered, "How do you know me?" Jesus told him how He had seen him under the tree.

This kind of attention hooked Nathanael onto Jesus. Who would want to leave a man who could look into your heart? It does not take a lot to notice the people around you.

How often do you really take time to look into their hearts? How much does it take to see the expression on someone's face, or to notice that they are not being themselves?

## *Get Involved*

You just do not want to get involved, do you? You see that someone is not acting like themselvers, but you think to yourself, "I am sure that they will figure out whatever is bothering them." And so, off you go on your own little track.

Well, are you the leader or are you not? If anyone should be getting involved... it is you!

It is not the way most of us have been brought up though, is it? For the most part, you do not know what to say if someone is not being themselves. Perhaps you know exactly what their problem is, but you feel ill-equipped to help.

Do you know what the best help is that you can offer? Love. Just get into their space.

## Break Down the Invisible Wall

You see, there is an invisible wall that we all put around ourselves. It is all mixed in with what we like to call our own personal space.

If you want people to follow you, then it is time that you break down the invisible wall.

You need to break down your own wall and theirs too. Think back on the last time you faced a personal struggle. You might not have wanted any advice, but you could surely have used someone who understood.

You wished that someone had the courage to just break through all of your nonsense and to love you anyway. When you are struggling with the flesh, you know you are messing up.

You know that you are in sin and you even know that you are going the wrong way. In it all though, you just wish someone could look past your grumpy exterior and love you – even though you do not deserve it.

When someone reaches out like that, it breaks down walls! Well, as the leader, you are the wall breaker. If you want people to follow you, it means getting into their personal space.

If it is clear that someone is having a bad day or is struggling with something, it only takes a moment to put a hand on their shoulder and say, "Are you doing okay? What is wrong today?"

As a leader sometimes it might even mean giving a correction, but the point is, you noticed! You got into their space and you did not let their struggle just pass you by as they crossed the room.

## The Power of Touch

I have found in personal experience that physical touch is powerful in this context. Is it any surprise that even when we pray for one another that we lay hands?

In this messed up world, I know that a lot of people can misread that, but I want to bring balance here. There is something about physical contact with someone that "puts you into their space."

You cannot help but break down emotional walls when you walk up to someone and put your hand on their shoulder. When someone is crying and you reach out and give them a reassuring hug that action means more than a thousand words.

Many leaders are so afraid of this though, but it is such a powerful hammer to those walls that people put up. I first learned this in an interesting set of circumstances.

### *Interesting Circumstances*

One of my spiritual daughters was pregnant and with it being her first child, she asked me to attend the birth. It was the first time that I was on the other side of the birthing table.

Her labor started and it began slowly. Eventually though the pains got worse and the staff left her to handle it pretty much alone. I felt in my spirit that I had to step in and become more involved.

I remembered what it was like for me the first time. You just have *no clue* what to expect. So, I reached out and put my hand on her shoulder. I rubbed her back and gave her reassuring squeezes on her hand.

There is something very precious about sharing a moment like that and when we left that hospital, our relationship had been transformed. I could have kept aloof, giving my great advice from the other side of the room, but I am grateful I decided to get involved and step past those walls.

There are people all around you pregnant with the visions, hopes, and dreams that God has given to them.

You can stand on the outside and bark orders, or you can get involved.

You can reach out with a reassuring hug or squeeze their hands to give comfort. You can be there to notice when the pains of life come at them.

Sometimes you will not have any words of comfort to give, because you know that these pains are something that they have to go through. However, you can stand by their side and see them through.

Not only will they follow you, but they will stick with you through thick and thin.

## A Note About Physical Contact

There are some guidelines that you can follow that will help you along this road. I find it easier to show physical affection to members of the same sex.

If you are going to hug members of the opposite sex, then it is good if your spouse or someone else is with you at the time. The Word says that we should be above reproach and in today's world it is sad, but true that many can misunderstand.

It is not a very fun subject to talk about, but if you know that someone is having a problem with lust, or if you struggle with this personally, it is best to just avoid physical touch, especially with members of the opposite sex, until you have gained victory in this area.

When we first came to the United States, we discovered what "huggers" they are! So, for the most part, it is not unusual to give someone a hug after we minister or when we greet.

In fact, in every culture, we all communicate best through both words and actions. A baby first gets to know its mother through touch and then only later understands the words.

Use this powerful medium with wisdom and do not be afraid to just reach out and put your hand on someone's shoulder. It will show that you care and that you notice and more often than not, that is the best ministry you can give.

## One-on-One Time

Having four natural kids and a lot more spiritual ones, this is one lesson I learned really quickly. Everyone needs to feel special to Mom and Dad.

Think about growing up. It does not matter how many siblings you had, you just wanted to be noticed. Unfortunately, this was not always the case and so you hoped that others would notice you and recognize you.

Even though you know that there are probably many others in the world with your skills or abilities, you still want to feel special. Well, when a child's need in this area is met, they rise up in confidence.

If there are people who are already following you, keep them at your side by noticing them.

## Building Relationships

Jesus spent a lot of time with His disciples but He also had one-on-one time with them. How do we know this? Well, because even when you read the gospels, you get a different perspective from each one.

We know that Jesus pulled Peter to the side to give him a piece of his mind. John was forever lying on His chest and having private conversations with Him.

There is only one thing more important than having a relationship with your team as a whole and that is having an intimate relationship with each one separately.

Think about your own relationship with the Lord. When do you feel that your own relationship with Jesus takes a big leap forward?

It is during the times when you are alone with Him or have received a personal revelation from Him. You did not develop a relationship with Jesus through your entire congregation at church.

No, it was only when you came to know Him one-on-one that you finally understood what your salvation meant.

Well, the people around you are no different. You cannot build an intimate relationship with a group. You can only build a relationship with a person.

This means one on-one time. It means taking time to get to know each person separately. That is why you have to be sure of your team and who you want a part of it, which is something I also cover later on.

I realized this myself when the Lord gave us our first spiritual kids. We always worked with everyone as a team. We took time out to have meetings and even to do social things together.

I noticed there was a problem when I saw that the team did not really seem to have relationships with one another. They all seemed to just have a relationship through Craig and I.

It felt a bit like because of their relationship with us that it lumped them all together. I realized that if Craig and I were not there to keep it together, there was no glue amongst them to keep things together when we were not around.

### *Get the Glue*

The disciples were not like this. They were so glued together that they could establish an entire movement after Jesus left. They sought one another out after He was crucified. Their relationship was not with Jesus alone, but with one another as well.

We realized that we had to start leading by example. So, Craig and I started to make time for each person individually. This way I could then teach them how to develop relationships with one another as well.

I did not want them hanging around just because they loved us alone, I wanted them there because they loved one another as well. Is this not what was said of the early church?

It was said that they were known because of their love for one another. When those around you love one another as much as they love you, they will follow you to the ends of the earth.

Not only will they have a place, but they will love the place they have. It will not be about who has the best job or the grandest title. They will continue walking because of the relationships that they have there.

Think about it! Relationships are the stuff that life is made up of. Why are you pushing forward with your plan or vision anyway? If you do not have the right relationships to fuel that vision, what is the point?

Is your objective to become famous, make money, and say that you did great? No, without people to share the exciting things God has given to us, there is no joy in doing the job.

Apostle Paul said so many times how he did his job because of his love for the churches. It was his love that drove him forward. Read his letters and notice the whole list of names that he gives.

Crazy, isn't it? Here he is reaching entire regions but he takes the time to mention the names of individuals who mean something to him. What an example!

Take the time to mention the individual names of those around you. Take the time to notice them. Take out some of your time to spend with them and train them personally.

Not only will they develop new skills, but they will start to think like you as well.

## 5. Replacing Yourself – Making Leaders

When we took the load of the ministry completely, it was not the first time that I had been put in charge. For years I had been given the opportunity to take and then relinquish the full load.

I remember though, the very first time my dad thrust the care of the ministry on me. He was the one who had given me the best example of how to raise a leader.

From the very beginning, he would give me a chance to take over the entire care of the ministry for a season. It took me many years and lots of tries before I was ready for the real thing.

It was one thing to be on the receiving end and another on the giving end though. The time came when I was the leader, and the Lord told me to give someone else a chance.

## A Chance to Sink or Swim

Craig and I had arranged a trip to Switzerland and Germany, which meant that someone else needed to take care of the ministry center while we were gone. Not only that, but we could not guarantee any internet access, so the entire work needed to be cared for.

Finances needed to be watched and bills needed to be paid. The children needed to be taken care of and the care of the bookshop and students needed to be handled.

The Lord told us to hand that care over to Ron and Denise. We were away for three weeks and were able to keep in touch with them in the duration.

However, the first week had not ended before we got a note from them saying, "We do not know how you do it. We realize that we are nowhere near ready to handle the entire load. We look forward to you coming back!"

By the time we returned they had both grown in leaps and bounds. They understood the load we often tried to explain to everyone.

## A Mile in Your Shoes

It is one thing to be under a leader, but it is another to take the load for a while. Nothing will gain the appreciation of someone more than letting them walk a mile in your shoes.

How often have you caught yourself saying, "Oh I can do that job better than him," when talking about another leader?

Well, do not be surprised to find that everyone around you has thought the same thing at one time or another. Okay, so what are you going to do about it? Defend yourself? No, I can think of something better to do. Why not give them a chance to do a better job than you?

They will learn quickly that it is not about the work you do, but the load you carry. I was no different. I always had a hundred things to tell my father when he was in charge of the ministry.

I always had a different way I would do things and there were even some times when I thought to myself, "Why is he making that decision? Surely there is an easier way."

It is very easy to talk when you are not in the driver's seat. When you are only responsible for yourself, it is too easy to have a big jaw and grand ideas.

However, when you are suddenly responsible for other people and one bad decision could mean crippling the ministry, your views change.

So, do as Jesus did. Do as I do. Give them a chance to sink or swim. Be there if they find themselves sinking like a stone but give them enough of the load to feel how heavy it really is.

Not only will it make them stronger, but you will earn their respect. Step by step, you will be replacing yourself.

This is the sad mistake that I see so many leaders make. When they cannot run the work, they try to get someone from the outside to do it, instead of trusting those who are right there under their noses.

Don't you realize that when you hand that care to them, you knit their hearts closer to you than ever before?

Before Peter was tempted, Jesus said to him, "When you are through, encourage your brothers." Later on, before He ascended, He followed Peter up again and said, "Feed my sheep."

Jesus was not afraid to hand over the work to Peter and to oversee it from above. If the King of Kings could trust a man with His most prized possession, don't you think you can do the same thing?

Did this make Peter want to go out and say how wonderful he was? No, the first thing he did was to reach out and tell the crippled man, "We do not have silver and gold, but what we have I am going to give you! In Jesus' name, rise and walk."

He did not talk about his own name or accomplishments. No, he gave honor to the one who had paid the price for him.

When you are a good leader, you do not need to be afraid that you will lose your honor. If you do, then you have failed as a leader in the first place.

## The Power of Expectation

Everyone hates expectation. Well, that is not entirely true. I have come to realize that expectation has the power to get people to follow you.

Does this sound contradictory? Well, think about it for a bit. What you really cannot stand is when expectation is put on you to do things you know you cannot do.

What you also hate is when someone always expects you to fail. In fact, you hate it so much that you will do everything in your power to do it right. Do you still think that expectation has no power?

So, how about you use that expectation as Jesus would use it? I made the mistake of thinking that expectation put on someone was just plain negative.

As my father trained me up, he had high expectation of me. I hated it! I always felt that he put more on me than I could handle. I was disciplined more than most and I was expected to do more than most.

What other people got away with, he never let me get away with. So, when I finally took his place in the ministry, I was determined that the very first thing I would change would be that whole "expectation" thing.

I vowed that I would never expect something of someone that they were not able to do. I vowed that if someone did not want to press forward, that I would not expect it of them.

I would not expect perfection and I would not expect them to be able to do everything that I could.

However, after some time I began to get frustrated with everyone. It felt as if they were always cutting corners. Their hearts were not in the ministry they were giving and if they let something slide by mistake, they did not seem to think it was a big deal.

After all, I did not expect it of them, so why live up to that *lack* of expectation? I started to wonder why I was the only one who pushed through.

Why was I the only one always making decisions? Why was I the only one always pushing myself to perfection? Why did I keep begging the Lord to take me from glory to glory?

What made me different to everyone else? I was not very happy with the answer that hit me right between the eyes.

When I looked back over the entire history of my ministry walk, I saw something profound. My father expected more of me than anyone else. I looked at the others that had come and gone through the years and saw that each one had reached a plateau.

## No Back Door

They came to a point where they got satisfied, or just plain gave up. I never had that option. There was never a "back door to escape" for me.

I had no choice but to push through. I did not have another country I could run away to. I did not have any other family that I could go and cry with.

No, there was no other option. I just had to change. I simply had to meet that expectation.

Then I started looking in the Word and I discovered that the Lord had an even greater expectation of me. He expected me to walk in His agape love.

He expected me to love my enemies. He expected me to walk in the spirit. He expected me to be holy as He is holy.

Wow! I had made a fatal mistake. I had let go of the power of expectation. The very thing I was so bitter about was in fact the power that qualified me as a leader.

As I write, I feel in the spirit that there are many reading this who have made this mistake in their lives;

not as leaders, but as followers. You had parents, teachers, pastors and so many others who put heavy loads on you.

They put expectations on you that you thought were unfair. So, you rebelled. You kicked and screamed and felt downright sorry for yourself.

What you do not see, child of God, is that these expectations were sent into your life to shape and change you. They were sent to transform you into the leader God has called you to be.

Instead though, you got bitter at God and at the authority over you. You failed to embrace the pressure that was meant to shape you.

Now you stand waiting to lead others and you are ready to let go of the very power that God needs you to use. You are too afraid to be bold, because of your own bitterness.

It is time to see the truth in this situation and to grow up a little. Look through your life and see the people who expected so much from you. Why did they expect it?

It was because they felt you had it to give! Tell me, why was my dad so tough on me? Why did he let others get away with stuff that I didn't?

Was he just being mean? No, not at all. He expected more of me, because he knew that I was capable of more. He expected me to think like him because he knew some of the road God had planned for me.

He knew the road that was up ahead, and he knew what I would need to become to walk that road. So, he piled on the expectation and only when I came to embrace and love it, did it begin to make me into a leader.

Only when I let go of my bitterness and stinky pride, could the Lord give me others who would follow me.

When all my anger was stripped away, I began to see that in my heart, I needed someone to expect something of me. I needed someone to see something in me that I never saw in myself.

## Expectation Based on Potential

As a leader that is for you to do also. It is for you to have an expectation based on the potential in each person you are working with. Set an expectation that is just beyond their reach, so that they will be forced to stretch forward and grow.

So, let go of the anger. In fact, start to praise the Lord for that load that was put onto you. Don't you see that it forced you to excel? It put you in a place where you were not satisfied to just be like everyone else.

It was this very expectation that forced your hand to step forward for God.

I ask you, how can you deny this privilege to anyone else? I had committed a great sin against my father, the Lord, and my team. I was bitter towards my father for all of the pressure. I was angry at the Lord for not letting me escape and I sinned against my team by not giving them the thing they really needed to grow.

When I changed this attitude, so did everyone else and I could transform my failure into success.

Let go of the anger! Let go of everything that is holding you back! In your memory return to the circumstances that still come up in your dreams. Take up the sword you dropped back then.

Embrace the pressure that you refused back then. Only when you do that, will you qualify to lead others. Only then will people want to follow you.

## Grounded in Love

Do you know that it is the very power of expectation that gets us up in the morning? It runs deeper than a desire to do something. It runs deeper than our feelings.

It is this power that forces a man out of bed in the early hours of the morning to go to work. It is this expectation that makes a mother work all day long and then still cook dinner for her family.

You see, when this expectation is grounded in love, you have a perfect mix.

We actually need this expectation to succeed in life. I thought that by just training my team and giving them a place was good enough. No, I needed more than that. I had to expect a bit more of them than they were able to do.

If I saw a skill to write, then I needed to expect them to develop that skill. If I invited them into my home, then I expected them to live by my rules.

When I released them to minister to others, I expected them to do it in faith, hope, and love and I made my expectations clear.

## Make Your Expectations Clear

I let them know that I expected them to be a part of this team. I expected them to commit 100% to the Lord and 100% to us. I expected them to love one another as Christ loved them.

I told them that there was no way to escape. There is only one door to walk through and it was the one that the Lord had for us together. I told them plainly that I was not allowing them to escape.

No running away! They would stay put, they would change, and they would allow God to flow through them.

I waited for the backlash. I was sure they would get mad! The opposite happened. It brought a peace and they felt secure. They realized that no matter how much they missed it, they always had a place.

If Craig and I expected so much of them, then it meant we would be there to follow through as well. It definitely increased the pressure, but it also made us stronger as a team.

You might be afraid to use expectation on those around you, because you have had so many bad experiences in your life. The key here is not to place your own expectation on them, but the Lord's.

That is really the balance in this subject. You cannot go around telling people what *you* expect of them. What you need to find out is what God wants and to expect *that* of them.

I can tell everyone boldly that I expect them to love one another as Christ loves them, because it is in the Word. I can say I expect them to minister in faith, hope and love.

I can tell them that I expect them to submit to my house rules, because the Word is clear on submission to authority. These are not my ideas. They are God's ideas and it is time that we expected the Church to abide by them, starting with the people around us.

## A Vote of Confidence

Once you have made your expectations clear, it is time to give a vote of confidence. The kinds of expectation that will cripple you are negative ones.

When Jesus was dying on the cross, He did not say to John, "John, I am giving you my mother to care for... please do not mess it up." No, there was no doubt in His mind that John was the perfect man for the job.

Give reasonable expectations and then a vote of confidence. One of my spiritual sons was going through prophetic training and was by far one of the most dramatic I had ever handled.

He was struggling and coming to a point where he just wanted to run away. It was this exact struggle that brought me to a true conviction on the power of expectation.

I got hold of him and I cut to the chase. I told him that there was no place to escape and that I was simply not giving him that option.

The pressure mounted and it seemed that the more he tried, the more he messed up. In fact, he messed up every job so badly that all we had left for him to do was to mow the lawn.

He was discouraged and swinging the pendulum wildly as only a prophet in training can do. He came to me one morning having failed with something again.

He knew what was expected of him and he had failed. One of the team had asked him for help with something specific late in the evening. He was tired and honestly did not feel like helping at all, so he made an excuse and went to bed.

He felt so convicted in the morning. He realized that he was not willing to serve. He knew that if the tables had been turned, the other team member would not have hesitated to help him. He came to me to talk about it.

I did not let him off that easy. I said to him, "Yes, you messed up, but you will never forget this lesson.

You will never make this mistake again because it is when you fail a test that you really pass and remember it. I know that right now you are messing up everywhere and you wonder if God can ever use you, but I want you to know that neither God nor we have given up.

You will pass through this training and you will rise up, because you simply have no choice. You will get through this and I expect you to not only become a strong leader but to rise up in the Lord's authority and power. So, you push through, because God will have His way."

I did not sugar-coat it and I made the expectation clear, but I also let him know that I expected him to succeed! It never crossed my mind that he would fail in his training. This gave him hope and while the rigors of training were tough, he had a new anchor to hold onto.

Give people a vote of confidence! Let them know that although you seem to be expecting a lot, that you do so because you can see that they have the potential to succeed. Then stand back and watch them rise up.

## Replacing Yourself

As you come to terms with the pressures that came on you to bring you where you are, you will be better equipped to train others, too.

Jesus said to the disciples that they would not only do the same miracles He did, but that they would do greater things! Again and again, He said that He only did what He saw the Father do.

In turn, He said that we should do what He did! Jesus came to this earth to duplicate Himself in us and this is why the Church keeps going from glory to glory.

This is the pattern for true leadership and when people realize that you have this kind of attitude, you will see them following behind you.

In the world and in the Church, there is always a limit of how high you can go, but do not follow that pattern in your ministry or vision. Let those around you know that they can have all that you have.

Let them know that all that God has given to you is also available to them. The sky is the limit! Not everyone will rise up to those heights and not everyone really wants to or should. However, when the option is open, they feel secure and they also have a goal to aim towards.

Who wouldn't follow a leader like that?

## Summary of Points 1-5

Perhaps it is because I am used to giving lectures that I like to put everything in point form, but before you catch the current of your journey and move onto the next chapter, I would like to bring everything together that you have learned so far.

Not only do you want people to follow you, but you want to keep them following. You can do that by applying these five powerful principles!

### 1. You do not need to know everything

- Acknowledge the wisdom and knowledge of others.

### 2. You do not need to do everything

- Hand out some "heart shares" in your vision.

### 3. You need to keep your fingers on the pulse

- Assume nothing!

### 4. You need to keep watch

- Break down the invisible walls.
- Dedicate some one-on-one time.

## 5. You need to replace yourself

- Give them a chance to sink or swim.
- Use the power of expectation grounded in love.
- Give them a vote of confidence.

## CHAPTER 08

# Winning the Heart of the Public

# Chapter 08 – Winning the Heart of the Public

We live in the era of the superstar. It was not much different in the days of David or Jesus though. Jesus was a little crazy, actually. It was what all the Pharisees thought anyways.

Here was this master teacher who obviously knew a thing or two about the Scriptures. However, instead of hobnobbing with the other scholars, he decided to spend his time with prostitutes and tax collectors.

The very thing that the Pharisees looked down on Him for, was the very characteristic that birthed the New Testament Church which is still going strong today. What did Jesus have that these other men did not?

Simply put, He was real! Why else do you think Jesus could talk about things that everyone understood? His parables were filled with the nitty-gritty of real everyday life. He knew it because He had lived there.

He knew what it was like to get his hands dirty and to work hard. Most importantly though, He did not forget any of it when He went into ministry. You get the idea that the Pharisees put all that stuff behind them to try and climb a super spiritual plain.

It was this very attitude that caused them to lose the hearts of the people and why Jesus could gain them.

Jesus could speak to someone poor or rich and win them.

So, what is the secret here and how can you use this principle to win the heart of the public? Well, take a lesson from our master, Jesus, the Son of Man.

## 1. The Reality of Who You Are

You know, Jesus could have gone by the title, "King of Kings." However, the Scriptures say that He put that title aside and took on the form of a servant and a man. He did not need His title to reach man, because He had something way more powerful than that.

### Identifying With People

And so, the first lesson you need to learn in dealing with people is learning to identify with them. You cannot do that if you are sitting on a pedestal trying so hard to get their respect. You think that if you tell people how great you are or how much you have accomplished that they will admire you.

Some might, but you will not win their hearts. They will likely say to you, "Well, that is easy for you. You had advantages that I did not."

If you want to win the hearts of the people, they need to know that you have been exactly where they are at, but that they do not have to stay there.

This was a challenge for me when I started my Esther Effect division. We always had many ladies coming to us for ministry and my dad suggested that I consider starting up a woman's site to give them some encouragement.

It is something that always burned in me, so I started out with just a few articles. It was a challenge because up until that point I had been the leader. I was the apostle and the woman behind the pulpit. What I needed to teach these ladies though had nothing to do with my position or title.

It had to do with being a woman, a wife, and mother. I needed to be something a lot more than just a preacher to do that. I had to be real.

So, I put aside my pulpit and my title and said it as it was. At first, I was a bit uncertain and thought that I might have been just a bit too real and open. I spoke about my marriage, giving birth to my children, and I even delved into very personal things like their sex lives.

What kind of response would I get? I must confess, I was a bit nervous. I wondered if by being so open I would lose respect or if it would have a negative effect on the rest of my ministry.

I could not have been more wrong! I was surprised at the influx of responses. Subscriptions poured in and before I knew it the list was a few thousand strong. The emails were passed from woman to woman and from church to church.

I did not realize the hunger the Church had for some reality. So many wrote in saying that these subjects are taboo in the Church, but how much they needed to hear the truth.

This is when I learned the important lesson of identifying with people. When I touched a part of their lives with mine, they let me into their hearts.

When they let me into their hearts, my message could reach and transform them. People won't follow you, until you win their hearts.

If all you have is a fancy story and super-duper revelations to share, they might follow you for the moment, just like they followed the Pharisees. However, when someone comes along who reaches their hearts, they will be quick to go there, because their needs will be met.

This is what Jesus had that the Pharisees did not, and it is your first step towards winning the heart of the public.

## Saying It Like It Is

By now you realize that I am not afraid to get into your face and be honest. I realized that even though we do not always like to hear the truth, deep down we really want to.

The great thing about public ministry is that you can be direct without putting someone under pressure. When you are working one-on-one with someone, you need tact. You need to be able to correct and reach them using a bit of wisdom.

You cannot just walk up to an individual and talk about their personal life right away. You cannot walk up to someone you know and point fingers at sensitive subjects like their marriage and personal sin.

You try doing that and they are out of the door! When you are ministering to the public though, you can easily do this! You can talk about sin and all the personal stuff you want to and still give your hearers a safe zone.

In a public meeting, people can decide whether that correction or personal revelation is for them or not. They do not feel on the spot and so they feel safe enough to receive what you are saying. Try saying that same thing face-to-face, and you will find a door slammed in front of you!

In a public meeting, you will find people are much more eager to receive from you if you say it like it is. Jesus was not afraid to publicly say what He thought. He told the Pharisees that they were whitewashed walls.

He whipped the money changers and told them that they were using the house of God as a den of thieves. However, consider how differently He handled Zaccheaus. He did not condemn the man of sin. Instead He told him that he would be dining with Him at his house. The Lord used a bit of tact with the man and as a result he repented and made a full turn around.

There is a time to get direct when dealing with someone one-on-one, but it is best to be led and use wisdom. You have so much more liberty in the public meeting.

In fact, you will find that people want and need it! They want someone to tell them the truth without sugar-coating it.

Consider John the Baptist. He was not afraid to stand up and condemn sin and say it like it is! As a result, people flocked to him. Once again, the Pharisees were jealous. Why is this? John broke out of the mold.

He opened his mouth and told the unadulterated truth. How did he get into trouble? He used that truth and confronted Herod and his new wife directly. In the end, it cost him his head.

I am not saying to avoid being direct when ministering to just one individual. I am saying that you will have better success being direct to the public. When doing one-on-one ministry, practice being as innocent as a dove and as wise as a serpent.

## No Fear – Be Bold and Courageous

How many times did the Lord have to tell this to Joshua? Why do you think that is? Well, how would you like to go up to a few million people and say, "Okay guys, let's have those foreskins out front and center please…"

Joshua had some tough jobs to do. Not only did he have to handle the load of leading the Israelites, but he also had to face the enemies who were ahead. He knew the giants were in the land and he knew how much the enemy wanted him dead.

His greatest struggle was not the enemy, but leading and organizing God's people. It is one thing to lead yourself, but it is another to lead others. This is why you need both, boldness and courage.

Is this not the same thing that Jesus told His disciples? There is a bit of a grey line here. I shared with you earlier how you need to be real. Many misunderstand this as being weak.

No, Jesus was never weak. Even stripped down naked and suffering on the cross, Jesus was both, bold and courageous. What is the difference?

The difference is that even though you should share openly what you have face, gone through, and struggled with, don't conclude without the victory!

There is no use in being open and sharing weaknesses that you have yet to overcome.

How will that help the people? Can you imagine Joshua telling the people, "Okay guys, the Lord has told us to walk around Jericho, but I must tell you, I am trembling here! I am not sure if we can do it!"

No, Joshua had his struggle before the angel came to him. He had his moment right there to overcome his fears. Once he was bold and confident in God's word he stepped out.

He could tell the men with strong conviction that they would win this war. Was Jesus any different? Did you think that just because He was the Son of God that He didn't struggle?

Consider the Garden of Gethsemane where He travailed and wept before the Father. He struggled, but by the time He was done, He had overcome and could face the cross with boldness and courage.

During this time, Jesus was alone with the Father. He did not even stay with His disciples. It was only after He gained the inner victory that He came out again and gave them direction and strength.

Jesus did not limp towards the cross in defeat. Jesus walked towards the cross with intention and boldness. This is why He won the hearts of the people.

You can do the same. There is nothing wrong with going through hard times. In fact, if you never went through hard times, I would doubt your calling!

There is nothing wrong with sharing openly what you have gone through, but when you do so, try to keep these points in mind:

**a. Share with intent.** Do not just tell stories for the sake of it. If you are going to relate something personal, do it for the purpose of ministering. Your disclosure should have a purpose.

**b. You should have already overcome.** Use illustrations from your life where you have already overcome so that you can give hope. You are not giving them any hope if you are counseling them on their marriage, for example, and you say, "Yes, I understand how you feel because I have the same problem in my own marriage…"

Do not be afraid to be real and strong in your convictions. David had a following because he was not only courageous, but also bold! If no one else wanted to fight Goliath, he was determined to do so alone.

He did not wait for people to agree with him before doing what he knew was right. He had what it took to jump in with boldness and conviction and when he looked behind him, people were following.

When people know where you have come from and see this courage in you, they will also want to follow. They will see that you have something they want. They will see what God has given to you.

Do not be afraid to be bold in your weakness and strong in His power.

## 2. Where the People Are

Sometimes we get so hung up on our own visions and ideas that we forget that not everyone lives in our little world. My daughters had the most fascinating way of playing growing up.

We never watched TV except for the odd movie but we also traveled a lot. So, the three of them were one another's best friends. They would go into a make-believe world and play out entire scenarios of their own invention.

They would get into their little world so much so that when I called them, I would have to do so for ages but they would not hear me. I had to get right up into their faces to get their attention!

When your heart is so on fire with what God is doing inside of you, you forget that a whole different world exists outside of you.

I can talk, because I am so guilty of this... I dare say guiltier than most. I get so passionate about what God is doing in my life that I can go off on a bunch of tangents at once.

Unfortunately, doing this pushes people away. I thought to myself, "This thing I believe in is so incredible, everyone must feel the same way!"

I learned that just because I was so passionate about something, did not mean others were as well. The same applies to you. What is so groundbreaking for you, might not be for others.

So, how can you swing it? How can you get them to become passionate about the same things you are?

## Part of a Greater Good

I saw this happen with my own children at a park. They were playing and I saw a little girl sitting by herself. So, I pulled the girls aside and said, "Why don't you go and invite that little girl to play? I am sure that she would like to meet new friends!"

They didn't need any further motivation. They marched on together and took the little girl under their wing to make her a part of their game. This then became a habit, and to this day, they are the first to notice the stragglers who do not seem to fit in.

You see, I gave them a cause. I gave them a reason to see things the right way. People need a cause and they need to feel as though they are a part of something bigger than themselves.

Just becoming part of your vision alone, won't inspire them. They need to feel that the part they play goes towards a greater goal.

I have covered this already speaking about working closely with people but this also works for public ministry.

David used this in the most powerful way. When he raided a Philistine camp, everyone in his army got a part of the spoils. It did not matter if they were in the fight or stayed behind with the baggage. As a result, these men followed him and his son, Solomon.

You cannot find that kind of loyalty easily in this world. David neither bought it nor demanded it, but he earned it by giving his men a cause.

However, It is important to know what the people want before you can give them a cause. For example, you cannot get people inspired about winning the lost, if they don't have this fire in their hearts.

This is why it is important to get some revelation. I do not know what I would do without the Lord's direction.

Like I said, because you are on fire, you think others share the same fire. No, you need to find something that they can relate to and are excited about. When you give them that cause, they will follow you anywhere!

## Being in the Know – Using Revelation

There are entire agencies in the world that dedicate all of their resources to watching market trends. They observe what trends are coming and going and then use this to advertise and invest their finances.

Well, as it so happens, we are in blood covenant with the very man who holds the world in the palm of His hand.

You can use natural means like taking a poll to find out what people want, or you can simply ask the Lord for revelation. By doing this, you take things out of the natural and into the spirit.

It is no longer a case of you wanting to manipulate people for your own ends, but rather about taking them in the direction God wants to lead.

Jesus did what He saw the Father do. He did not tell the disciples to do only what He wanted because He thought it was a good idea. When you go to the Lord with the intention of getting revelation to lead His people, He will surely give you wisdom.

This is the kind of wisdom that Solomon had. He knew what to say and where to lead and so the people followed him towards that success.

You can receive the same wisdom from the Lord. How often though have you tried to "figure out" what people want in your flesh?

Well, what is your motivation? Is your motivation to try and manipulate them into doing what you want, or do you truly want to lead them in what God wants?

As a leader you should be spending time daily before the Lord asking Him about His plans for His people.

When you do this, the heavens will open, and you will receive the revelation you have been looking for. Have you been asking the Lord for new revelation for your preaching?

Have you been struggling to flow in the spirit or get fresh ideas? The problem is likely not the revelation, but your motivation for it. Do you want to receive that revelation for the sake of the people or for your own sake?

I have just seen too many leaders receive a revelation only to say, "Do you see my great revelation? Aren't I something? I am so close to God!"

## Love the Work of the Ministry

I can talk, because I have been there. When my dad handed the ministry to me I felt myself in a corner. The Lord used him in incredible ways and the way that he flowed in revelation was unlike anything else I had seen in the Church.

When he handed the ministry to Craig and me, I felt that I had to fill those shoes. I had this crazy idea that suddenly I had to flow in the same kind of revelation otherwise I was not good enough.

So, I tried. I strove, struggled, and cried out to God but at the end I just fell flat.

I finally got to the point of crying out to God, "Lord! I cannot do it! I have failed somehow because I cannot get this kind of revelation."

The Lord replied, "Who said you had to?"

Good question! No one said I had to flow like that. It was just my own idea. It was a load I had put onto myself. I had convinced myself that unless I could get earth-shattering revelation, I was not good enough.

I felt a bit like an idiot when the Lord pointed it out to me. I had spent so much time striving after something I did not need to!

So, I let it go. I said, "Okay Lord. Here I am. If all I need to be is a clanging symbol for you, then so be it. Forget about the fancy messages. I am just going to bless your people."

Two things happened when I came to the end of myself. For the first time in ages I started to love ministry again.

For the longest time it had just been such a grind. I felt as if I was always falling short and not good enough. When I dropped that wrong motivation, I continued with what I loved to do.

I motivated and encouraged God's people. I wrote articles and I ministered one-on-one. I saw lives change and I saw new doors open.

In the middle of it though, I noticed one day that something miraculous was starting to happen. The revelation had begun to flow again.

I was having so much fun just ministering out of my heart that I did not even notice that the Lord had started to put new pictures in my spirit.

The revelation I had tried so hard to receive started to bubble up from inside my spirit naturally and as it was needed. I got it when the people needed it.

I got it when I wanted what the people needed.

Learn this lesson now and you will find joy in ministry again. Spend your time trying to get revelation for the sake of it and you will always come up short.

## 3. Leading the People Forward

Once you have won the hearts of the people and you have given them a cause, you need to tell them how to get there.

The second book I wrote was *Practical Prophetic Ministry*[j] and in my mind it was one of the best works I had ever completed. I felt the Lord's hand on me so strongly when I wrote that and today it is our top seller. However, it did not start out that way.

I was so excited after I had written it. I thought that everyone would want a copy! I could not wait for it to be announced! Instead of people knocking down our doors though, things were slow.

I could not believe it! Why would they not want this book? Could they not see that they needed it?

## Building Trust First

Well, why should they believe me? Why should they believe me when I said this would launch them into their prophetic training? Who was I?

At the time I was just a 27-year-old who had written a few lessons on the prophetic. My dad once again came to my rescue and recommended I start a mailing list and offer a free prophetic course.

He suggested that I start by winning the people and giving them an idea of the kind of things I taught. It was a good idea and I went straight to work.

We set up the www.prophetic-network.com website and I started writing. I loved it! This kind of thing was up my alley and I just poured out what I had at the time.

Once again, the list grew like crazy, and soon became one of our most popular. The biggest surprise though was not the quick growth, but the change in the hearts of the people.

They began to trust me! The teachings I gave there touched their hearts, and so when I suggested to someone, "Listen, I think you should get your hands on the *Practical Prophetic Ministry*[ii] book..." they did!

I could not believe it! All this time, I knew that they needed it and that it would answer their questions, but they only listened to me now.

What made the difference? They trusted me! When I suggested that book, they knew it was because I wanted to bless them. It was not just because I wanted to make a sale.

How often do you feel that you are being "sold" in the Church? Whether you are being sold on a new idea or on a new book, no one likes it!

However, you are quick to act, if a friend comes up to you and says, "Hey, I tried this new thing out. I think you will like it!"

Why? Well, they are your friend and they have your best interests at heart. Do you have the people's best interests at heart? Are you giving them direction because you think it is good for them, or good for you?

When you can get this straight, you will win people and they will follow your instruction.

What are you giving the people that makes them trust you?

Are you being transparent and real?

Do you really care about what God wants for them?

When you have true concern and the people trust you, they will follow you when you lead.

## Confidence to Give Direction

They might trust you now, but do you have the courage to lead and give direction?

It actually took me quite some time before I had the courage to say to someone, "Please go and buy my book." It just sounded so self-serving. The Lord challenged me though. He said to me, "Do they need this book? Are you telling them to get it out of love?"

I said, "Yes Lord. They really do!"

He told me that while I was wavering in giving them direction that there were many others in the world and Church who were not afraid to give the wrong direction. While I was waiting, the people followed the wrong direction instead.

Would I prefer that they read my book or one that led them into deception?

Well, that sure made up my mind fast! I suddenly did not care what people thought my motivations were. They needed what I had! I would rather come across wrong and snatch them out of the fire than keep quiet and see them be led as sheep to the slaughter.

There comes a time when you have to stand up and be bold in the direction that you give. You cannot skirt around the issues and when it comes to public ministry, you have a lot of liberty to do that.

Look at the people around you. Do they need something you or someone else has? Do not be afraid to tell them that they need it.

Rather they follow a direction that will lead them to green pastures and still waters, than a direction that will lead them towards the butcher's house.

## The Power of Appreciation

People like to be remembered. Craig and I have a favorite restaurant in Mexico and there are a number of reasons we return there as often as we can. They serve fresh salsa made from oven roasted tomatoes and garlic, hand mixed with a mortar and pestle, right by your table.

The prices are good, and their tortillas are handmade in an oven that is in the middle of the restaurant. The main reason we return though is because of the owner. It is a family owned place and the owner pays personal attention to all of his guests.

They are not his customers, but his friends. He remembers your face, name, and the last time you visited. After being away for a long time Craig and I stole an evening away there for some alone time. He tucked us away into a private corner. Then, he brought a specially prepared liver and onion appetizer (on the house), because he knew it was one of Craig's favorites.

do you feel as if you are a customer at work? You come in, you do what is expected and you leave.

You do not feel that you belong unless you have something to offer. So, why bother? Why follow and why give your heart? Well, look around you! That is the way people all over the world feel too.

Once you have motivated them for a cause and they have followed you, do you remember their names and their birthdays?

Do you remember that their kid was sick or that their marriage was going through a hard time? It is tough sometimes as a leader. I wonder how many times the owner of that restaurant received a gift, or if any of his patrons ever asked him in earnest how he was doing?

It is a tough job, but if you want people to follow, then it is for you to both lead and follow up. It does not take much time to notice and care, but it will keep the hearts of the people.

Public praise is probably one of the most powerful tools you can use, and it gains the respect of everyone who follows you. It takes a mature leader to step aside and give someone else a moment in the glory.

Moses was never afraid to push Joshua forward. Moses was not afraid to give Aaron a place of honor, either! David was also amazing in this area.

Even though Saul wanted to kill him, he was not afraid to give the man honor. He was not afraid to step aside and give someone else the spotlight. As a result, his men followed.

When was the last time you gave praise and honor to others? When did you last show your appreciation to the people? These gestures are so simple, but so powerful as well.

## Giving Recognition Publically

It does not cost a lot to give a bit of your heart to others, but it sure means the world to them. I have a very dedicated team who work hard.

There are very few who actually see what they do. They see Craig and I stand up and preach the word. People attend our seminars, and everything is taken care of. They do not see how much hard work and heart went into it.

When I stand up and give each of my team praise, it does not cause them to turn their backs on me. Instead it knits their hearts closer to me. Not only that, but I also gain the respect of the people.

It does not steal from my leadership, but adds to it. This was a powerful lesson that I learned as I rose up through the ranks myself. My father was never afraid to push me forward and to give me a chance.

As a result, when the day came for me to lead I could rise up. No matter how much God uses me though, I know why I am here. I know who poured everything into me. I might not be able to hang onto his coat-tails anymore, but the respect will always be there.

Win the hearts of the people by giving them your own first. Not only will they follow you to where God is leading, but the Lord will also empower you with both the revelation and anointing that you need to get them there.

---

[i] Toach, Colette. *Practical Prophetic Ministry: The Metamorphosis of the Prophet.* 3rd ed. San Diego, California: Apostolic Movement International LLC, 2016

[ii] Toach, Colette. *Practical Prophetic Ministry: The Metamorphosis of the Prophet.* 3rd ed. San Diego, California: Apostolic Movement International LLC, 2016

**CHAPTER 09**

# Following the Ark

# Chapter 09 – Following the Ark

There is nothing more daunting than taking a trip to a place that you have never been to before. This is especially true if it is in a country that you have never been to before. This is something that Craig and I have had a lot of experience with.

When you are driving in a country you have never been to before with so many unfamiliar roads, it really helps to have someone who can go ahead of you and lead the way. Even someone with a GPS can help.

Imagine that whole you are following the guy along the curved roads you get this great idea.

You think, "You know what? I think that if we take a different turn-off, it will be a shorter route." So, you radio the guy up ahead and say, "I think we should take this turn-off."

The guy up ahead says, "No, I know where I am going, just follow me."

But you decide to take the turn-off anyway and the next thing you know, no one is around. You find yourself in the deep, dark jungles of the inner city.

You do not know where you are going, and you have never been there before.

Everyone in town is looking at you strangely as you wander around. There you are, driving up and down, all the while thinking, "Lord, why didn't I just keep in line with the car in front of me? It would have been so much easier."

Instead of heading to your destination, here you are, going around the same landmark for the 50th time.

Joshua had a very clear command from the Lord when it came time for them to cross the Jordan.

> ***Joshua 3:3-4*** *And they commanded the people, saying, "When you see the ark of the covenant of the Lord your God, and the priests, the Levites, bearing it, then you shall set out from your place and go after it.*
>
> *4 Yet there shall be a space between you and it, about two thousand cubits by measure. Do not come near it, that you may know the way by which you must go, **for you have not passed this way before.***

The Lord told the Israelites that He was going to take them to the Promised Land. He said He was taking them to a land that they had never been to before. This was God's plan and vision for them.

"I am going to lead you across the Jordan, but this is how we are going to do it. I am going to set my ark a distance in front of you. We are going to have the lead group of Levites up ahead.

The reason I am doing this, is so that you can have a clear sight of them, because you do not know this territory! You do not know whether to go left or right. So, I am going to be your GPS here. All you need to do is watch the Ark."

## Watch the Ark

It could not have been any simpler. Just like the children of Israel, you too have a vision of your Promised Land. You have the promises that God has given to you.

The Israelites ended up wandering in the wilderness for a while, but they knew all along that the promise and the vision were real.

God has given you a vision and a hope and even though you have faced some storms and dry times, that vision has remained. You are finally coming to a point in your life where you feel something happening.

You are seeing things happening in your circumstances and God has started to open the way. After all the training and pressure, you are starting to see some signs of life.

It is just like the time when God came to Joshua and said, "Now is the time to cross the Jordan." So even now the call has come to you in your spiritual walk and the Lord has said, "No more wilderness. The waiting time is over! It is time to put your keys into the ignition and to follow me.

However, if you are going to reach your destination, then you need to watch the Ark."

This is what will make or break your vision. Where are you at right now? Perhaps you are a little impatient. You have waited so long for God to do what He said He would do.

You know that God has called you and that He has a plan. Yet every time you tried to step forward you would hit your head against a wall. However, now things are changing, and you are impatient.

You have prepared yourself. You have studied and you have gone through the pressures that have given you some new character traits. If you had to think about it, you have become quite comfortable with the road you have been walking on.

Sure, there has been a bit of fire along the way and a couple of things that you had to face in the wilderness. Even though it was a tough time, you learned to handle it.

You've learned to overcome your struggles. On the one hand you are nervous and on the other hand, you feel that you can do this thing.

You feel ready. Well, you will find out soon enough if you are ready to take your step across the Jordan.

There are a few things though that you might not be aware of right now.

## You Have Never Been This Way Before

The first thing you need to realize is that you have not been this way before. You have become comfortable in the wilderness and you have come to rely on your own strengths. Whether those strengths are natural, spiritual, or social, you have come to lean heavily on them.

However, this is a new road that requires new skills. You can no longer rely on what you had before. This will take a whole new level of dependence on the Lord.

Everything is about to become unfamiliar. Even though this is a vision that you have been trusting God for, the way is new to you. I can imagine that the Israelites must have lain in bed at night picturing what the Promised Land would look like.

However, the only one who had seen it before was Abraham and he did not paint a picture of what it was like there. And so, they might have imagined what it would be like, but they had never seen, touched, or tasted it. All they had was a promise.

## Death of a Vision

Unfortunately, us humans can get a bit bold and arrogant. You think that you have the entire vision in hand and you just want God to open the way so that you can make it happen with your own will.

Sure, you can bring this vision to pass, but only if you watch the Ark. Only if you follow God's direction in His time and in His way. Perhaps you have come this way before. For the Israelites this was not the first time that they faced the opportunity of going into the Promised Land.

Do you remember what happened the time before? The Lord brought them to the land and instead of watching the Ark, they watched their circumstances and said, "Lord, we cannot do this! No way."

So, the Lord said, "Okay, no way it is then. We will put the Ark on hold and wait a little while for you guys to die off so I can work with people who really mean business."

Instant death of a vision!

As if that was not bad enough yet… they decided to take things into their own hands after they realized they had missed God. Suddenly they realized that God was right, and so they tried to run ahead and take the land.

It did not work out so well though. They fell flat on their faces. They messed up badly, because they did not follow God's lead. First, they dragged their feet, and then they tried to run ahead of the Ark and tried to do it themselves.

Perhaps you have faced a few of these situations in your own life. Sure, your vision is real. God told you that you would go this way. Do not forget that it is on His terms, however, because you have not been this way before.

It is not on your terms. This means that when the Ark goes two paces, you go two paces. When the Ark stops, you stop. If you can watch and follow the Ark, taking it a step at a time, then you will accomplish the vision God has given to you.

Perhaps you have had your ministry and vision die one death after the other. Over time you got bitter and angry at God. It is not God's fault that you did not watch the Ark or follow in His perfect timing.

By His grace you are getting another opportunity from the Lord. And so, you stand as Joshua did: ready, eager, and excited about the hope that God has given.

## How Will You Follow?

How will you follow the Ark? How will you get it right this time? How will you make sure that you can make it along this journey where others before you failed?

Well, by the end of this chapter, you will know exactly what it will take.

## Do Not Run Ahead of the Ark

You see, this is what the Israelites did when they tried to take the land without God. It goes back to my illustration of the convoy of cars with the lead car setting the pace.

The car behind the lead car thinks that they are going too slowly for their liking. So they put their foot on the gas and overtake.

So… now you are going double the speed. Double the speed to where though? You are going double the speed to nowhere! This is what happens when you become overconfident in yourself.

"Oh yes! I know what God wanted. Of course! I can think five steps ahead of the Lord."

So, you just jump ahead and off you go. Being an expressive, I find myself in that boat often. Sometimes when Craig is driving, he will notice that the traffic is a bit congested. So he will think to himself, "I am going to take a different route today."

Sitting alongside him, I am watching and thinking five steps ahead of him (of course). I say, "Craig, you need to take that lane over there."

"Love, I have this under control."

"But… if you do not take this lane you will miss your turn-off!"

"I am not going that way today. If you were quiet and waited for five minutes, you would have noticed that!"

How many times do you treat God that way?

"God, I know that you said the Promised Land was over there, but I think you missed the turn-off. Lord, I think you need to open this particular door. This is looking so good for me right now. I *really* need you to open this door!"

"I've got it under control."

"Lord, do you need some help with the door? I can see you are busy… Let me help. You know what? I can see you are tied up. Let me just take care of that door for you…"

And so, you try to shove and push that door open. Then you turn around and discover that the Lord is no longer there. Suddenly, the opportunity falls through.

You would think that you would have learned your lesson after the first time, but instead you try to push against the closed door. All you are doing though, is hitting your head against that closed door.

All the while the Lord is standing 200 paces up ahead of you saying, "Can we please move forward now? When you have finished hitting your head against this closed door, I have a paved, wide open road for you here."

Yet you keep insisting on the doors you must go through instead of letting God lead. The more you push and run ahead, the worse it gets. You think to yourself,

"Wow! The call of leadership is so stressful. This fivefold ministry call is so tough! It is just one death after the other."

Well, no surprise there! It is stressful because you are being stupid. God did not want you to go through that door that is why it did not open. It is quite logical actually. So, let it go.

Perhaps there is a door that He wants to open, but something else needs to happen first. Joshua could not defeat Jericho before crossing the Jordan. The reason is obvious: Jericho was on the other side. The Jordan came first.

There is a natural order of things for your life too. Perhaps that door is for another time. Watch the Ark for His timing and His way.

It is miraculous what happens when you do that. The Ark moves forward into the middle of the Jordan and the waters just stop. This should be an easy walk.

Do you know what happens if you try and jump across the Jordan before the Ark gets there? The Scripture says that the river was in high flood. You try taking a leap like that and you are going down!

"Whoops. There goes old Bob into the water again. See ya later buddy... we're crossing the Jordan."

You will get swept away because you did not wait for God to stop the waters. Then you cry out to God, "Lord, why am I drowning here?"

"Well look, I just do not know how to make this any easier for you. Watch the Ark! Wait for me to stop the water. Wait for me to open the doors."

You see there is a time for action. I am getting to that point next, but I do not think that is the main problem most folks have.

Most people have this problem of jumping ahead of God. They are so busy diving into the Jordan that they forget to wait for the Ark to stop the water.

So, if you feel like you are drowning and the enemy is destroying you, perhaps you are wondering where you missed it. Actually, it's only when someone is mature that they wonder where they missed it.

Most people say, "God really missed it."

## God's Way Is Easy

If you take time to wait for the opportunities to present themselves, when you then walk through them, it will be such a rest. You do not need to bang doors down.

You do not need to cry out to God all of the time and "shake the gates of heaven." You do not need to throw a tantrum and intercede for hours at a time.

You do not need to even push through on your own, because the Word says that the Lord puts before us an open door that no man can shut.

If you are walking in step with Him, He will present you with opportunities as you walk along. Your eyes will be opened to see the circumstances around you. You will feel the clear leading of the Lord in a specific direction.

Even though you might have the natural tendency to go in one direction, you will see activity in a different direction. Then you will know that this is the direction the Ark is going in. The people could only walk once the water stopped.

The Lord did not say, "Alright everyone, I have a swimming lesson for you today. I need you to learn some backstroke. Then, just dive in and push, push, push!

Don't worry if you lose men along the way. I know it is in high flood and most of you will die! But hey, at least some of you will make it through!"

No, God is not in the business of leading you to an open door only to drown you. God made it easy for them. He stopped the water. And so, here you are psyching yourself up to face the Jordan that is ahead of you, thinking you must face death, travail, wilderness and pain.

Listen, there does not have to be any pain! When you do things God's way, there is no pain. Perhaps the reason you have had so much pain is because you did not watch the Ark.

The Scripture says that the Lord's burden is easy and His yoke is light. When you do things God's way, then it is an easy walk. There will always be death to the flesh. There will always be circumstances that will feel like Jericho in front of you.

However, when you do it God's way, those walls will come crumbling down without you having to set so much as a hand on one brick! That's God's way.

When things are done in His power, He moves, and you follow. When you follow like this, you release such a power into this earth. You give God license in your life to do things that are unimaginable.

Who could have imagined the power that God used to bring Jericho down? They were ready to take the land by force, but the first thing God told them to do was to rest.

He started them off with a simple fitness routine, doing a few laps around the walls of Jericho. They took a nice Sunday stroll, and God took care of the walls.

God sent the Ark around Jericho and all they had to do was follow it. God brought the walls down then, and He will also bring the walls down in your circumstances.

He will bring about miracles, will tear down the enemy and build you up. He will open doors on your behalf and give you the land that He has promised you!

# Chapter 10

# Crossing the Jordan

# Chapter 10 – Crossing the Jordan

## Taking Action at the Jordan

God gave Joshua a clear command and the priests went ahead into the Jordan. Right before their eyes, the Jordan stopped.

You get those who lag behind when God gives a new direction. There are always a few of those around in every group.

What would have happened if a few of the children of Israel were too afraid to cross the Jordan when God stopped it?

What if they took one look at the water and said, "Hmm, I don't know. That is a whole lot of water going on there in the Jordan. I am just not sure if I am ready for that.

I have a bit of a water phobia and I had a really bad experience with water as a child. I am just not so sure I can face the Jordan right now, Lord. Rather come back for me later!"

The Lord has opened up one opportunity after the other for you and there you sit waiting for God to do something. Can't you see that the Jordan has stopped? There is dry land ahead of you. A miracle has taken place in your life.

God has moved and shaken the earth on your behalf. Instead of moving forward you think to yourself, "I know that there is something that I should be doing here…" but you never take any action and do it!

It reminds me of that old story about a man who is caught in a flood. He is stuck on a roof and calls to God to save Him.

Along comes one boat after the other, but each time they come, he says, "No, go on ahead! God will save me!" A helicopter comes by and tries to save him, but still he does not get on board, insisting that God will save him.

Eventually the water overpowers him, and he drowns. He went to heaven and asked, "Lord why did you let me drown?" The Lord answered him by saying, "I sent you a couple of boats and a helicopter! What more did you want from me?"

## Change the Picture

Unfortunately, you have a picture in your mind of what God has called you to do and before you take a step, you want a full map. You want the full picture before you step out.

You want the Lord to tell you how to cross the Jordan, take down Jericho, the first land for you to conquer and with how many people… all before you take the first step.

Well, no wonder you have been hiking around the wilderness for so many years. I have more news for you… get used to the taste of sand in your food, because you will be staying there for another 40 years.

## Time to Walk

When God opens a door, it is time for you to walk. There is a time to wait as well. When the Ark stops then you stop. However, when it moves, you must move with it. If the waters of the Jordan dry up, then it is time to cross over.

If people start to call you out of nowhere or opportunities for ministry start coming to you out of the blue, this is a sign that God is moving. Now is not the time to wonder what you should do.

You have been waiting for years for this opportunity! It is what you have been nagging God about for so many years. You have cried out again and again for God to do something. Then, when God suddenly gives you five open doors, you wonder if they are God's will.

Short of coming out of heaven and shaking you, what more of a sign do you want? I can imagine that God must get very frustrated with us sometimes.

## Do Not Miss Your Open Door

The problem with not taking the opportunity when it comes is that those opportunities can change. Times change and the Ark is moving. Either you are going in step with the Ark or you miss your time of visitation.

You will miss this open door and will wander around that same mountain again. God, through His grace though, will open other doors for you. Unfortunately though, there was a door you missed at the very beginning.

God has opened up many doors for you, but do you know what the big problem is? Often you are waiting for that first door to open again.

## A Second Chance

The original spies who went out under Moses missed God and that opportunity to enter the land, came and went for them. They never entered into God's promise.

In the same way you are still waiting for that first opportunity to come knocking again. Let me help you through this process. Let it go! The door is gone and lost. It is part of history and the circumstances have changed.

Times and plans have changed. God has moved on. The Ark has moved on without you. You are being given a second opportunity for a new destination, but that first destination is gone.

You will spend the next 40 years wondering why God has not opened the door, when in fact He has. He has just not opened the door you want.

Perhaps like the children of Israel, you realized that you missed God and you try to go back in your own strength to take the land. You think that perhaps God will open the door now. However, what did God tell the children of Israel after they had missed Him?

He told them that under no circumstances would they see that land. If you missed an opportunity some time ago and failed, I have no words of comfort for you except: Deal with it.

## Deal With It. Let It Go!

For as long as you hold onto the past and the old doors that you missed, you will miss the huge welcome sign to the new open door that God has for you now. You will miss it continually.

Leave it behind. Take your eyes off your failures and the doors that you missed. Here is a reality: We are human and we fail. God also knows that we fail which is why we rely on His grace and love.

If you missed an open door, it will never be made available to you again. Let it go. God has another open door for you with something more fantastic. Be open for new circumstances and signs all around you!

You are so busy looking behind you that you do not see the Ark in front of you. You will end up going the wrong way. Let go of the mistakes and failures and the times when you missed God.

## God Is Bigger Than Your Mistakes

God is bigger than your mistakes and your failures. He has long forgotten about them, so it is about time you do too.

There is a job to be done in the Church. God has a plan for your life. It is time to move on with that vision and not lag behind any longer.

Joshua only got his full direction concerning Jericho after he had crossed the Jordan. You won't get the whole plan ahead of time.

If you tend to be analytical and need the whole picture, you will struggle with this one. Take it one step at a time. Get across the Jordan first.

Walk through the first open door. Take the first opportunity that presents itself to you. Do not just sit there and think yourself out of an opportunity.

You are so busy thinking about your opportunity and what this will mean to other opportunities that you lose out completely.

You will tie yourself up in knots and miss God's perfect time. When you see a circumstance taking place that is out of the ordinary and you cannot deny that God did something, then it is time to stand up and to move forward.

If you do not take that opportunity with all that is inside of you, it will pass you by.

And so, we are starting to see a balance here.

Do not run ahead of God and decide to race the Ark to Jericho. On the other hand, when He opens a door, get up and walk through it with everything that is in you.

If God has given you a direction, then it is time to work hard and push through. Do not sit around thinking about how wonderful the direction is and then end up doing nothing. Now is your time to run!

As you take that step, you will see that God is in control. After you have taken your first step, the second will follow quickly.

Revelation and circumstances will suddenly come into line. As you take the one opportunity, you will suddenly bump into people and it will open other doors.

One thing will lead to another and more doors will open. It will be like a domino effect. However, if you keep hitting wall after wall, then you are not going through open doors that God has given to you. Become aware of your circumstances and take it slowly.

## The Picture Becomes Clearer

As the Israelites stepped over the Jordan and took Jericho, they started to get a clearer picture of the land that they were going to possess.

They started getting a clear idea of how they were going to defeat their enemies.

## The Two Mistakes to Avoid:

### 1. Do not wait for the full picture first.

You will never get the full picture first. If you got it that way, you would think up a few points of interest to add where you feel God forgot a few things.

It gives the enemy too much license to mess with the plan. God will give it to you a step at a time. If God could do this for Moses, Joshua, and Paul, then you and I are in good company.

### 2. Running ahead and trying to take the land alone.

If you do not follow the Lord, you will miss your opportunity. Keep your eyes fixed on the Ark and take a step at a time.

## Assess Yourself

Where are you at right now in your leadership walk?

### Has God given you any promises?

I want you to consider all the promises and visions that God has given to you over the years. Make a list of them!

### Has God opened any doors for you?

Consider your circumstances right now. Is there any new revelation that He has given to you lately?

Have you perhaps suddenly run into something new? Have you been given a new responsibility lately?

Look for things out of the ordinary. Look for a specific theme that keeps coming at you from all directions.

**Have you received any new visions lately?**

If you can identify with all of these points, then can you see that God is opening some doors for you?

Perhaps you have a clear picture of what God has called you to and now a door has opened up to you. Unfortunately though, it looks nothing like you expected it to.

You want to go right, but this door opens to your left. God knows something that you do not and although this door seems strange to you, if you walk through it, He will lead you to the perfect destination.

It might not make sense to you, but He sees something that you do not. He sees the problems and the obstacles that you do not. And so, to get to your destination, you might need to take a route that is longer, but it will take you there.

So, what are you going to trust? Are you going to trust the Lord? Even though the door He has opened seems foreign, have faith that He knows better. In the end it will lead to where you must go.

Is God opening up doors for you? Have you been given jobs to do? Have you applied yourself to these things and put your heart into them 100%?

If that is where you are right now, then you know what to do. It is time to step forward.

What do you do if you are one of those whom God has put in a place to wait?

It is time for you to get quiet in His presence. It is time for silence so you can hear His voice and get revelation. Perhaps you are one of those who are hitting their head against the wall, pushing in a direction God did not lead.

Stop and wait until you see the Ark once again. Wait for the revelation to come. Do you know what is funny? An open door could be staring you right in the face, but you are so busy running around that you do not see it.

The ram could be caught right there in the thicket. You would see it if you only stopped your striving for five minutes to see what God is doing.

Perhaps there is no open door ahead of you right now. Perhaps God wants this time for you and Him and there are some things that you need to learn for your journey. It could be that you are a couple of tools short on your toolbelt.

You need to get them before you are ready for this journey. Enjoy the rest while you can. Before you know it, this season of rest will be over, and you will be up and running again. Then, you will long for that moment of rest.

Just up ahead of you is the Promised Land. He has promised that you will overcome and that you will get your inheritance. Take your step across the Jordan in boldness.

Then you will see God doing things in your life that you did not think were possible.

## PART 02: BECOMING A PERSON PEOPLE WANT TO FOLLOW

**CHAPTER 11**

# Don't Scuttle Your Ship

**PART 02: BECOMING A PERSON PEOPLE WANT TO FOLLOW**

# Chapter 11 – Don't Scuttle Your Ship

## The Price You Never Think About

I remember one of the toughest tests that I faced just a short while before we took over A.M.I. We had been working with a large group of people in Europe.

I had personally worked quite extensively with many of them, spending hours a day in personal counsel and encouragement. However, the situation changed, and the main leader there decided to separate from us.

We stepped aside and allowed the rest of the group to follow. I was devastated. I felt rejected and the need in my own heart rose up so strongly.

I started to feel resentment. I felt that they owed me so much. After all I had done, this is the way they treated me!

I wished I had not given so much of my heart and time. I started to back off from others that still stuck close to me, because I was afraid, they would treat me like that as well.

I had a good rant and rave and after a little while, my dad came to me and said, "Colette, if this is what the Lord wants, are you prepared to do it? If it means going through this continually for His sake, are you prepared to do it?"

I felt the struggle in myself. I felt like I was waging a war between my own flesh and what I knew the Lord wanted. I can imagine what Moses must have felt like when the Lord told him to return to Egypt.

Why should he go back to those Israelites? They did not embrace him. The Egyptians rejected him. What was the point? And so, just as Moses struggled with God, so did I.

It was not long though and I knew that there was really no choice to make. Without the Lord and the call on my life I was an empty shell. The fire for Him burned more strongly in me than the rejection and my own deep need.

So, I let go and died to that fleshly struggle. I said, "Okay Lord, I will do it. If it means rising up and ministering again only to be rejected, I will do it. If it means that I keep pouring out without any recognition or receiving any love back, I will do it."

Something broke in me that day and I knew I had somehow passed a test. From that time on, not only did the Lord begin to open doors again for me, but through that He started to bring healing.

## Healing Will Come

What this entire situation did was expose a very big need in my life. One that I thought I had dealt with. I have come to find in my own experience that the Lord likes to deal with our needs in layers.

It's as if He deals with what we are able to bear at the time. Peter was not ready for the full truth that Jesus had for him just before the crucifixion. The Lord told him that he would be tested, but it was only as he worked through that test that Jesus could bring the healing and promotion.

Only after Peter saw the fear and struggle in his heart, could he receive healing for it. That fear had been there all along, but it took a particular circumstance to bring it up.

So, do not be surprised when with the first step you take forward in your leadership, something happens to rattle you and expose all the nasty hurts from your past.

## Taking an Axe to Your Ship

I cannot think of a better picture to illustrate what I mean than sharing a childhood moment with you. As a teenager I had a passion for comic books. My absolute all-time favorite was a series called, "Asterix and Obelix."

If you are in the United States, you might not be too familiar with this series, but I just loved them! In fact, do yourself a favor and get hold of one, because they are a huge laugh.

If you are familiar with this series, you know that there is a certain group of characters that show up sooner or later in every story. I am referring to the little pirate ship. You just have to feel sorry for this poor group of pirates.

I say that because each time you meet them in the story, as they are out at sea simply doing their "pirate thing" they come across the heroes of the series, Asterix and Obelix. If you know the story you know what happens each time they meet.

Those poor pirates get a good beating and their ship sinks every time. One story stands out to me though. In this one, the pirates see Asterix and Obelix coming on the horizon. So, the captain of the ship takes an axe and starts chopping up his own ship, causing it to sink.

His crew tried to stop him and said, "Are you nuts? What are you doing?" The captain replied, "Forget trying to escape! I am scuttling my own ship before they do it for me."

## A Sure-Fire Way to Sink Your Ship

Let me tell you, there is one thing that will scuttle your ship every time. In fact, it is like taking an axe in your hand and chopping a big hole in your ship, sinking yourself to the bottom of the ocean.

So, what is this one thing that is a sure way to sink your ship? The answer is simple – neediness!

We will look at this a little bit, because neediness is one huge axe, sinking your ship.

You can have goals, ambitions, and hopes. You might have the "plan of all plans" but you still can't figure out why people do not want to follow you.

It is because you are just too needy. So, let's look at this and move onto dealing with it so that you can get your ship to its destination.

We have covered this particular subject in so many books that I am going to skim over it and refer you to teachings such as *The Crucified Life*[iii].

## Where the Need for Acceptance Comes From

Firstly, being driven by an unmet need for acceptance stems originally from having a bad relationship with your mother growing up. We have covered this subject in a lot of detail elsewhere with full scriptural reference. So, I will just give you the bottom line.

I want you to think back on your school days. Think back on the kids who seemed to just have it all together. The select few that everyone liked. The people you even liked. I guarantee that every single one of them had parents who were involved in the school and in their lives.

They had a good relationship with their mother. Perhaps you saw their mother pick them up from school each day, whereas you had to always catch the bus or cycle home in the cold.

I sure hope that I am not triggering too many bad memories here! You looked at those kids and said, "Those lucky kids!" They had mothers who actually cared and attended all their games.

As a result, they were confident in themselves. As a result, you wanted to be around those kinds of people. Everyone did. You thought to yourself, "What do they have that I do not? What makes them so popular and special?"

The answer is simple. They knew who they were. They were confident in themselves and because of that you wanted to follow. For everyone else who did not have this experience in life, does this mean that you are stuck now?

You did not have this kind of relationship with your mother, and you have all this neediness inside of you, but now you want to take your vision and accomplish everything God wants you to. What are you going to do about it?

Well, the good news is you can do something about it. Just as there is one sure way to scuttle your ship, there is also one sure way to deal with this need inside of you correctly. *The answer is found in a face-to-face relationship with Jesus.*

There is no man, woman, child, or animal in this world who can fully meet that need inside of you. You might have tried to reach out in so many ways to get that need met. Perhaps you have reached out to your spouse, children, friends, pets, and parents to get that need met.

What happened? Perhaps for a short moment in your life that need was met, but people will always let you down. People move on. Friends move to a new house. Dogs die. That's life. No one can meet that need forever.

You might find someone to meet that need for a little while, but sooner or later, you will say or do something that will upset people. They will react making you feel rejected. When that happens, the need comes up again and you feel sorry for yourself.

## The Ultimate Solution

There you are, at the bottom of the ocean again. There is only one person in this world who will understand why you are full of rubbish. There is someone who will understand you even when you fail 100 times.

He will always say, "Well done," and will find the one tiny thing you did right in the mountain of things that you seriously messed up.

His name is Jesus. I cannot go into full detail here on how to develop this relationship, but I cover it in my book *The Way of Dreams and Visions*[iv] if you want more of the Lord.

Jesus cannot only meet that need but reverse its effects in your life. He can literally go back in time and undo the mess that your parents made. He can undo the mistakes that you have made.

**Your very first step is realizing that:**

1. No one in this world can fill that need inside of you.
2. The only solution to that need is Jesus Christ.

I am not condemning you for having that need, because every single one of us has it to some degree. However, where are you trying to get it met?

If you are trying to get it met in other people, then let me tell you, you won't make it to the front of the line for others to follow. In fact, you won't even make it out of the harbor before you sink!

You will be scuttling your own ship. You cannot keep blaming others for not following you, using that as an excuse because you did not achieve your vision.

No, it is your fault for holding onto that need that chased them away. Let me reiterate this point. *If people are not following you, it is not their fault for not following.* Rather, it is your fault for not being the kind of leader that they want to follow.

## Nobody Wants to Be Your Solution

And so, you are sinking your own ship by so desperately needing others to accept you and to say, "Wow! You are doing so great!" No one wants to be anyone else's solution in life.

Take a look at the Lord Jesus. He said:

> **John 2:24-25** *But Jesus did not commit Himself to them, because He knew all men,*
>
> *25 and had no need that anyone should testify of man, for He knew what was in man.*

Think about it. While He was on earth, how many times did He ask His disciples, "Was that okay guys? That sermon on the mount... do you think I came across too strong?"

Jesus was not only confident in Himself, but He came to give of Himself 100%. You can only be in that place when that need inside of you is met.

You can try to convince me by saying that you are trying to have other orientation and that you are trying to meet the needs of others.

However, while you still have that need inside, you cannot try and cover it over and think that if you are nice to everyone all the time that it will make you a better leader.

No, the truth is that having other-orientation stems from a point of already having that need met. When you know who you are in the Lord and your need for acceptance is met then it is natural to really notice and listen to people. Only then will you naturally want to pour out to them.

When you are confident and filled up inside then you naturally want to flow out. You cannot try to act your way out of this.

## What It Takes Away

What does this neediness take away from you? Firstly, it takes away your confidence and your conviction. You can believe something so strongly without a doubt, when you are alone in your bedroom where no one is watching.

Then you step out into the world with your big mouth (okay prophets... I am especially talking to you here). You step out with your great expectations and your, "Thus saith the Lord!" What happens though?

Everyone steps on you and says, "Who do you think you are? That word is not from God!" How do you respond when that happens? Your conviction goes right down the drain. Maybe inside you still have a conviction, but because of the pressure, you start compromising.

You start conforming and pretending that you are someone else. You try to say what you feel you should in such a way that people will accept you and so lose your conviction.

## Why Did I Start This Road?

The goal that I shared about in the first four chapters starts to become really fuzzy. You do not see where you are headed anymore. You wonder why you started on this road in the first place.

If you are currently at the point in your spiritual life where you are asking the Lord why you took the direction you have, then you need to consider that you compromised your conviction.

You have forgotten the direction God has given to you. Why? It is because of the neediness inside of you. The first time that someone opposed you, you were swayed by it. You started to think that perhaps you did not have a clear picture. You began to doubt if you heard God clearly, or if He perhaps meant something different.

If you are called to the work of the ministry you are headed for a difficult phase in your spiritual walk called, "death of a vision." This is because you are killing the vision God has given to you!

## Neediness Takes Away Your Goal

You are trying to change the vision God has given you by fittin it into what everyone else is saying to you. This is what neediness produces. It takes away the clear sight of your goal.

Instead of trying to blaze a trail like God originally told you, you add things from others. You start to do things like the status quo, when you know clearly that God has called you to step out and do something that no one else has done.

When that need is so great inside of you, you are too afraid to step out and do something no one else has done. And so, you compromise. You take some of the things on board that people are more likely to accept to try and smooth your message over. You try to become politically correct instead of saying it like it is.

## Polluted Vision

Your vision becomes polluted. It gets polluted with the ways of the status quo and with the ways of the world. Then you cannot understand why your vision is dying. Yet you have taken an axe and scuttled your ship.

Your neediness steals the life out of you. Do not allow it to destroy what God has given to you. Can you see how we are coming back to the same point? It is not everyone else's fault that you failed.

It is not your pastor's fault because they did not like your message. It is not your brother's fault because he thinks you are crazy. It is not your friend's fault because they think you are flaky.

It is your fault for allowing such a deep need in your heart to sway you. You have lost hold of the precious gem of a vision that God has given to you.

If you want people to follow, you need to make it a priority to deal with this problem in your life. This is why the fivefold ministry is needed in the Church. The body of Christ needs to become mature and not be swayed by every wind and doctrine.

## Bringing Maturity to the Church

If you are called to the ministry, don't you think it is a good idea to begin by maturing yourself before bringing maturity to the Church?

You cannot teach others how not to be swayed by the heretics out there without looking at yourself first.

You might have some great ideas, but with that need in your heart driving you, the enemy will use it continually to sway you from God's purpose for you. The minute you face opposition, you will fall down.

You become like the children of Israel who went around the same point again and again. You come to the Lord for a vision, but yet, each time you lay it down because of the opposition you faced.

Are you confident of the vision God has given to you? Are you sure of the destination and the goal? If it is a bit fuzzy for you, and you notice that at one time you knew for sure, but now you feel uncertain, then you need to take a look at your heart.

Perhaps you have allowed others to demotivate you. Perhaps you have allowed others to tear at the conviction God has given to you. It is time to go back to basics and to stir the fire afresh.

It is time to get back to your convictions and to stand up in boldness once again.

---

[iii] Toach, Colette. *The Crucified Life.* MP3 file. San Diego, California: Apostolic Movement International LLC, 2015

[iv] Toach, Colette. *The Way of Dreams and Visions: Interpreting Your Secret Conversion with God.* 3rd ed. San Diego, California: Apostolic Movement International LLC, 2016

## Chapter 12

# Becoming Confident

# Chapter 12 – Becoming Confident

The perfect image of confidence is what Jesus looked like when he boldly stood in front of his followers and said:

> **John 6:53** *Then Jesus said to them, Most assuredly, I say to you, unless you eat the flesh of the Son of Man and drink His blood, you have no life in you.*

It says further in John 6:66-68 that from that time, many of His disciples were no longer associated with Him. After that, Jesus turned to His twelve and said, "Will you also go away?"

However, Simon Peter replied, "Lord, to whom will we go? You have the rhema words of eternal life."

This is someone who doesn't just know his convictions but is also not afraid to stand in them. When you deal with all the need in your life correctly, you can stand in strong conviction and you won't move away from what God told you to do.

You won't be afraid to say the truth as it is. Jesus was not afraid to face the Pharisees and say to their faces, "You whitewashed tomb! You are filled with dead man's bones!" On the other hand, He was also not afraid to say to the woman caught in adultery, "You are forgiven of your sin. Go and sin no more!"

He said it like it was. He was not afraid to open His mouth and speak the truth. Consider how you act in a group or fellowship. Are you really confident enough to say what you think, even when you know that you won't get the response that you want?

If you are not secure in yourself, you will dance around the point, trying to pick out the right words and smooth things over with every word you speak, every message you bring, and every meeting you hold.

You try to pour oil on troubled waters, trying to make everyone happy and keeping everything nice.

Do you know what though? I do not want to make everything nice. I do not want to make everyone happy. I want to make them uncomfortable. I want to shake them and rattle the foundation of the Church until everyone's teeth start to shake!

I want the Church to start seeing the truth as God sees it instead of the pretty paintings and plastered walls that have become so popular.

## Getting a Reaction

I want to shake the Church so much that the plaster drops off the wall, so that the children of God can rise up without being swayed by every wind of doctrine. However, nothing will change until you have the courage to stand up and speak the truth.

If you are afraid, you will keep trying to smooth things over. You will be afraid that others won't like it.

Well, that is the idea! Honestly, I do not want you to like what I say.

I do not want you to think that what I have to say is nice. No! I want to challenge you and I want to anger you. I want you to throw something at me and say, "You are annoying me."

Praise the Lord! I am getting a reaction! If I am not getting a reaction, then I am not doing my job properly.

People follow leaders like that. We see ordinary people like the "girl next door" every day. No one is following a person like that.

## Be Louder Than the Others

So, tell me again, what sets you apart? If you have the courage to stand up and say what needs to be said, then you are louder than the others. You will shine more than others. You might get shot down a few times, but for everyone that shoots you down, another ten will follow.

Sure, not everyone will follow. Sorry to bring you some reality. Not everyone in this world will say, "Wow! What a great man (or woman) of God." There are a lot of people who like the plastered walls, the whitewashing, and the stained glass windows.

However, for everyone who likes the stained glass windows, there are ten others saying, "I am sick of things the way they are." The Church will stay the way it is, until someone has the courage to stand up.

We need leaders in the body of Christ who are secure in themselves and do not have neediness. We need leaders like Jesus, who after hundreds of years of the Pharisees being in control and putting burdens on God's people, stood up and removed those burdens from them.

Sure, He faced a lot of rejection. So much so that they put Him on a cross, put thorns on His head, and pierced Him in the side. However, even today the Church of God continues to thrive. Every minute of every day, the Church continues to grow. He has reached so many from that single act of love.

## Deal With It! Rejection Will Come

Rejection will come. Deal with it! Not everyone in this world is going to be nice to you or love your message. That is life.

You see, if you do not have that desperate need for acceptance pushing you, not only will moments of rejection have no effect on you, but you will be able to see where they are coming from. You will be able to love them as Jesus loved them and to die for them as Jesus died for them.

When you are secure in yourself as Jesus was, you do not care who follows and who does not. Jesus did not care that the Pharisees wanted to wring the life out of Him. After all those disciples up and left Him after He challenged them about drinking His blood, He was so secure in Himself that He could turn to the twelve and ask them if they were leaving as well.

It reminds me of when Elijah told Elisha to remain behind while he made his journey up the hill. Elijah's attitude was, "If you want to come along, fine, but do not do me any favors. Whether you join me or not does not matter. I am going!

However, if you decide to come along, then you will certainly reap the rewards."

## Don't Just Accept Anyone

Jesus had such confidence. He continually challenged those who came to him. So much so that at times, He even purposefully pushed them away. And so, He tested His disciples in this way.

He did not just take on anyone who came to Him. In fact, He spent a full night in prayer in the presence of the Father before He chose His twelve disciples.

Not everyone who called Jesus "Master" was immediately chosen to be a part of the twelve. You see in the Scripture how Jesus tested those who came to Him. When James and John came and asked Him,

"Master, show us where you stay," Jesus replied, "Let me show you where I stay."

However, there were others who came asking the same thing to which Jesus responded, "Foxes have holes and birds of the air have nests, but the Son of Man has nowhere to lay His head." (Matt 8:20) In other words, "Go away. I do not have any place for you to see."

Jesus was very selective in who He accepted into His team. He was confident and because of that, He could hear the voice of the Father as clear as a pin dropping in the spirit.

If you do not have this kind of confidence, you will have people following you and becoming part of your team who will end up tearing you down and destroying the vision God has given to you.

If you are so desperate for people to like you and like your vision, there will always be at least one person who agrees with everything you say.

However, is *this* the kind of person who should be on your team? Is this the kind of person God wants to be on your team?

You will always get someone who likes you and compliments every message you preach. They will share how much they are applying what you teach to their lives and you will be tempted to think, "This is a team leader in the making! This is someone who loves me and appreciates what God has put into me." Do they really?

## Finding Your Mighty Men

Many appreciated what Jesus had until He started putting pressure on them. Everyone appreciated what David had when he was under Saul slaying his ten thousand, but where were these people when David was running for his life?

Did either the dancing women, or the clan leaders follow David to the cave of Adullam? No, not at all. It is wonderful while you are looking good. Then the praise is heaped on you.

However, when the pressure is on, where are they then? The Word says that when David ran to the cave of Adullam, the outcasts and his family joined him. They then became his mighty men.

David was not needy. It was clear that whoever wanted to follow him had to believe in what God had given to him. Furthermore, they also had to pay a price of they wanted to be a part of his mighty men.

You should have that same attitude. Do not just accept anyone. When you start developing this attitude, you become extremely valuable.

This is one of the greatest mistakes so many leaders make. Just because someone is nice to you and complimenting you all the time, you think they are wonderful. They said that of Jesus too as He rode into Jerusalem. In unison they sang, "Hosanna, blessed is the King of Israel that comes in the name of the Lord!"

A short while later though that same crowd sang a different heavy metal tune. It went along the lines of, "Crucify Him!"

## What Kind of Team Do You Want?

What kind of team do you want? Do you have a clear picture of what you want from your team? When you are secure in yourself, not only do you have a clear picture of what you want, but you are also not afraid to make demands.

You are not afraid to test them to see if they are really the kind of team member you want as a part of your vision. I already showed you that you need to firstly know where you are going and secondly what you will do when you get there. With this in mind, you should have a clear picture of the kind of people you will need to participate in this vision.

When someone comes along who does not even come close to what God has given to you, but always says what you want to hear, are you swayed by this? If you make them a part of your team just because they flatter you, you won't accomplish your vision in the end.

What is the point of moving forward? Is it not to do what God has told you to do? If so, then you better look for the kind of people who will help you get there. Do not be afraid to say that "this" is what you expect of your team.

Do not just accept anyone. Jesus did not accept just anyone to be part of the twelve and even when He selected them, He took His time. He never said, "Anyone can come and live with me." He tested everyone who followed Him continually.

Then, even after the twelve were chosen, He continued to test them! Jesus was not afraid to put pressure on them. Do you think that was unreasonable? If so, take a good look at what happened after Jesus was resurrected.

A church was born on the Day of Pentecost as Peter stood in boldness. In a single day the Lord ushered 3000 men into the Kingdom of God! From that point, the Church was added to daily.

## The Right Man for the Job

How was this possible? It is because Jesus chose the right man for the job. He put more pressure on Peter than on the others. Peter failed the Lord gloriously and even in that Jesus was testing him.

Each time Peter passed those tests he continued to push through. As a result, he became the kind of man who started a move that brought the Church into the glory that continues even today.

Jesus did not choose any old guy who flattered Him and called Him, "Master." There were many of those.

Be selective and do not be afraid to test. Ask yourself, "Do I really want this person as a part of my team?" Once they become part of your team, you will give them everything you have.

You will give them your time, your vision, and even your very life. Before they are accepted as a part of your team, they should be prepared to pay the same price you did.

Jesus looked at His disciples and knew He would die for them. He said to them, "Unless you are prepared to forsake mother, father, and all you own for me, you are not qualified to be my disciples."

Do you think you have it tough? Jesus was clear about what He expected of His twelve and His demands were high. He called them to give up their family, lands, and all possessions. (Mark 10:29) How did Peter respond? He said, "We have given up all these things to follow you."

Jesus responded, "Yes! Because of this you will receive a hundred times and will inherit everlasting life." (Matt 19:29)

## Guard Your Pearls

Jesus in return gave up everything for them. Before you hand out the pearls that God has given you to just anyone, be sure that those people are prepared to pay the same price.

If Jesus, the son of God, laid down such a standard for His team, should you not be doing the same? Rather be like Jesus, instead of being so grateful that someone wants to hear your message and then accepting them just because you have such a need to preach.

You may think that accepting just anyone will gather lots of people to you, but it won't. When you no longer have a desperate need to minister or have people compliment you, you become the kind of person others get their needs met in.

Even though you might try to cover up your needs, people will still pick it up. Humans are very perceptive. They can sense neediness in the same way a dog can sniff out a piece of steak.

When they sense that, they run a mile! People do not want to be around you. Again, no one wants to be the solution to your problem.

## A Little Secret

Becoming confident is not something that just happens to you. As you have read through this chapter perhaps you see some of that insecurity in yourself.

You are beginning to see that your need is so big and also that you are insecure around others. Instead of pouring out and being objective, you keep being swayed.

So, how can you overcome? The Lord taught me a little principle that got me started on the right road towards confidence. I will end this chapter with it and arm you with a little secret that will wipe away your insecurity as if it never existed.

## Using Your Point of Strength

Years back, when I first went into full-time ministry, I was only 22-years-old and although I was passionate behind the pulpit, I felt really insecure when I came down from it.

I shied away from people within a group and, believe it or not, I was quiet and unsure of what to say. It was not that I had nothing to say, I just could not find the words.

My mind was always so filled with what people thought of me that I could never work past that to really minister to their needs.

I cried out to the Lord and asked Him to save me. I was hoping that He would swoop down and just make me into something else.

Well, I guess in a way He did, but I had a little bit of work to do first myself.

The Lord made me think about the times I felt most secure. That was obvious. When I was under the anointing or behind the pulpit, I did not care what anyone thought. I was not representing myself there, but the Lord.

It made it easy for me to stand up tall. The Lord said to me, "Alright, it is simple then. When you find yourself in a position of weakness, imagine yourself in your point of strength."

In other words, when I was in that social gathering or that situation where I felt so insecure, all I had to do was imagine that I was standing behind the pulpit talking for the Lord.

I gave it a try. When I was at a social event and tempted to think about what everyone thought about me, I imagined myself behind the pulpit instead.

I imagined that I was speaking to them on behalf of the Lord and that they needed what I had. Something miraculous happened. I had taken my eyes off myself and put them on the people.

Suddenly, a bubbling came up from inside. I became expressive and I could reach people. I was so busy looking at them and their needs that I had even forgotten I was feeling insecure.

It took me some time to master this and as I was learning I was probably a bit too super spiritual for most. After all, you cannot develop a relationship with someone who is always behind the pulpit.

However, by using my point of strength in my place of weakness, I stepped past my own fears. I learned to pour out.

Between that and developing my personal relationship with the Lord Jesus, I changed. I won't forget the day I woke up and suddenly realized that the deep aching need inside of me was just not there anymore.

I cannot tell you the day it left completely, or the exact moment when the Lord fully healed me of all those hurts from the past. The point is though, I was so busy pouring out and wanting the Lord to use me that I plain forgot about my hurts.

In that process, as I was pouring out healing to others, God had come and healed me.

Do you need healing right now? Can you think of a place where you feel insecure? Where is it that you would rather hide? The Lord wants to transform you and make you confident.

Start by standing in your point of strength, when you feel the weakest. Develop that personal relationship with Jesus until you know how much He loves you. The change won't come overnight, but it will be miraculous when it happens.

You just keep pouring out to God's people. Continue to heal them and to let that anointing pour through you. As their hurts are healed and as their needs are met, the Lord will meet yours as well.

God has called you to be bold and confident and He will give you what you need to become that kind of leader. Put Him at the helm and when He is in charge, your ship will always be in safe waters.

## CHAPTER 13

# First Stage of Leadership Training: Servanthood

# Chapter 13 – First Stage of Leadership Training: Servanthood

## How a Leader Is Made

I was in my teens when I signed up as a waitress at a local steakhouse. I had to wear this awful uniform that included braces (you know those things that hold up your pants). I had a cap on with my hair neatly tucked inside, leaving my ears hanging out of it.

As strange as it may seem, this was the moment in my life when I learned a secret to becoming a leader. (Also, just by the way, it was around the time when Craig and I met for the first time.) So, there I was with my denim jeans, my really dorky looking uniform learning my first lesson in leadership. How did I learn a lesson in leadership being a waitress?

Very simply put, I learned to be a servant. Let me tell you, there is no greater servant than a waitress in a restaurant… Especially in a family restaurant where kids and a host of tables demand your time.

"I want one of these please, and one of those."

"Why is my steak cold?"

"Why isn't it cooked properly?" (As if you were the one behind the grill making the steak.)

"I'm sorry, sir, I will see to it that it's taken care of right away."

"Why did you burn my steak? Why did you do 'this'?"

You can only say, "Well, I'll go and sort that out for you."

I tell you, you have to learn. You can't jump in there and say, "Then cook your own steak!"

I mean, you want to say that… but you can't. You hold back, smile sweetly and reply, "I am sorry about that sir. I will sort it out for you right away".

It was tough and for an expressive like myself, I had to learn to bite my tongue. And so, I learned to serve. Through a process of a few months and of dealing with the public, something began to happen. I suddenly didn't have to grit my teeth anymore.

I suddenly realized, "If I came to a restaurant and a waitress spilled the entire glass of soda all over my lap, I wouldn't tip her either."

I came to understand my customers a little more. As I learned to serve, I realized that there was a joy in serving.

I didn't stay there though. One day my knight in shining armor came along carrying his own tray. He stomped in there with his pair of braces. Sporting his own cap, he swept me off my feet, married me, and the next thing you knew, we landed in Mexico with two small children.

The first stage of leadership is summed up beautifully in this passage:

> ***Philippians 2:7*** *But made Himself of no reputation, taking the form of a bondservant, and coming in the likeness of men.*

Here is Jesus, the King of Kings, Lord of Lords, but He came to this earth having put aside His deity. He laid aside His royalty and came as a mere man. He came and took on the role of a servant.

Can you see it? There is Jesus with His braces on saying, "Alright, what have we got here today? We've got five thousand loaves and fishes coming on up…"

He learned to be a waiter, too. He was dishing out fish and bread. He was there to serve the people and He gave of Himself all the time.

## Launching up the Leadership Ladder

As you look at becoming a leader and getting others to follow you, it is time to look ahead. Rising up to become that leader is much like climbing a ladder.

There are clear steps for you to take and as you take them, you will reach the top. As you rise up, you will stand tall and be seen by men. As you climb higher, your vision and ministry will grow.

So, I want you to see the leadership ladder standing right in front you, because you will launch up that ladder until you reach the top rung.

However, do you know where you are right now? Do you know what your starting point is? Well, do you see that rung right at the bottom?

From where you are standing right now, that rung is a promotion for you!

Guess what? You won't even reach the first rung until you learn to be a servant.

Perhaps you have prayed the fatal words, "Use me Lord!" If you did, then you can rest assured that He didn't just hear you, but already started to bring pressure on you.

## The First Stage of Leadership Training

### Servanthood

Have you cried out, "Lord, I want to be a leader?"

Fantastic! The first thing that He will do is strip you of everything. He will strip you of every leadership role you have had, along with all your titles and everything you were nice and cozy with. When He is done, you will be stuck somewhere cleaning dishes all day.

You started out with great ideas of leadership, but now you find yourself stuck somewhere between vacuuming the floor for the meeting and answering the phones in the office.

"Oh yeah! I'm in ministry now, baby! Cleaning the floors... cleaning out the toilets. Glorious!"

When Craig and I first arrived in Mexico, he was the gardener. Oh yes, he really served the Lord in an apostolic capacity... with the weeds in the backyard, for days on end.

However, if you want to be launched up the leadership ladder, this is such a vital part of your training and is indeed the first step.

If you are wondering why you haven't had a promotion, or why you have never progressed past that first plateau yet, it is because you never got on the first rung of the ladder.

You haven't even gone through the first stage.

I love this scripture:

> **Mark 10:44** *And whoever of you desires to be first shall be slave of all.*

Just do a search in the Scriptures for the word "servant", and you will see how many times it occurs in the New Testament alone.

The question is, are you prepared to be humbled? Are you prepared to let go and serve?

There are many who say, "Yes Lord, I am your servant, send me to the nations and I will humbly stand before millions of people and give them your word."

How very humble of you! Thank you for sacrificing your life.

Jesus did His main work in the early hours of the morning, slaving away with His disciples hour after hour. He did His work by pouring out, giving, and being rejected without a moment's rest.

We did not get the gospels from the multitudes that He preached to, but from the individuals who knew and loved Him.

When we use the term "servant of God" we think that we get a title and an exalted position.

You get something alright! You get a broom, a rake, and a spade. That's what you get.

## How to Become a Leader

I love Luke 17:7. It speaks about the servant who works in the field all day long. After he worked hard in the field and comes in, the Master does not say, "Hey buddy! Take a seat. Have a drink and feed yourself."

No, after the servant worked all day in the fields, he comes in and makes the master's food. Only then, once the master has been fed and has been given his bath and is nice and cozy in bed, can the servant go and eat.

That doesn't seem fair at all, does it?

It says in the tenth verse:

> *So likewise you, when you have done all those things which you are commanded, say, We are unprofitable servants. We have done what was our duty to do.*

You see, it's not good enough to say, "Well, I worked hard, Lord! I did your work. I cleaned the toilets. I watched the kids and I did all the other jobs."

## The Servant's Heart

Yes, but what heart did you do it with? It is all about your heart. Do you have a servant's heart?

After serving everyone around you, do you think that they should be very grateful for what you have done?

You feel in your heart, "This ministry owes me a badge for the work that I have done and the hours that I have put in!"

That's not really a servant's heart, is it?

"I deserve apostleship at the very least for all the work I have done here!"

That's not the heart of a servant either.

A servant's heart does everything that was expected and then goes beyond that. Then after doing all that they say, "What are you giving me praise for? I've only done what is my duty to do."

Are you prepared to put aside all of your titles, settle down, and do the jobs nobody else wants to do? Furthermore, are you prepared to do them with joy?

Or, do you perhaps feel that things like that are below you?

Jesus bent down to wash His disciples' feet. Jesus took care and fed the multitudes when they came. They didn't have to nag him for food. He saw that they were hungry, and He said, "Come, let me feed you."

Did He, as the King of Kings, have to feed them? Did He even have to care that they didn't pack a picnic lunch?

Yet, here was the master caring about the children, women, and men. Here He was, concerned over the fact that they were hungry.

## Where Nobody Sees

Are you prepared to look after the little things and to offer somebody of a lower rank than you that you will take care of something, instead of making them do it?

If you can, that is the heart of a real servant. A real servant is somebody who serves when nobody is looking.

In our passage in Luke, the master doesn't see how much work the servant does in the field. Yet, the servant still does it with joy, knowing that he is doing it as unto the Lord.

## Taking a Lower Seat

Are you prepared to step back and give others a place of honor?

Blessed are the poor in spirit for the Kingdom of heaven is theirs. Go and read that some time! You will read that blessed are those who are hungry because they will be fed, and that blessed are those who are thirsty because they will be given something to drink.

Well, blessed are those who serve. Blessed are those who take the lower seat. Blessed are those who are secure enough in themselves to let go, because then they will be raised up.

After all this, when you are finally given that place of honor, it will be a glorious day.

## You Will Be Launched

When the time finally comes and you have your position, you will know you don't deserve it. Secondly, you will realize that you do not need to put yourself in that position. It will be handed to you. You will discover that you didn't have to climb the ladder yourself. Rather, you were launched up the ladder.

This is the point I am trying to make here. You don't climb up the leadership ladder with your own effort. If you walk the way correctly, you will be launched there by the Holy Spirit.

If you are prepared to say, "Lord, you know the desire of my heart, but I'll serve. Even if it means that nobody ever knows my name. Even if it means that nobody sees what I have done except you. I am prepared to do it."

## Miraculous Change

When you get to this point, a miraculous change will start to take place.

Just when you think that you will always be the servant and be pushed to the background, something will happen. When you are content in this place, the Holy Spirit will step in and lead you to a higher seat.

I look at the example of my stepmom, and the price that she paid.

Many look at her now and they see what a tremendous example she is. They didn't see her when we first started out together in ministry. The Lord released me into prophetic office ahead of her, and so a time came when I had to mentor her into the prophetic.

How humbling is that?

She cooked for us every evening because we were staying in their home. She did the dishes every day. She would get up in the early hours of the morning when my children knocked on her door saying, "Granny, we want tea!"

She didn't yell and say, "You horrible little kids! Go ask your mother." Instead, she would get up, make them tea and breakfast.

However, as she was prepared to keep that position, God raised her up. When that happened, I don't know who was more surprised, her or everybody else.

She didn't raise herself up. She didn't stand up and say, "Here I am guys! Look at me."

She didn't have to say it because God raised her up and set her as a mother to the nations. God did what she couldn't do.

## What the First Stage Forges in You

What is one of the greatest things that we admire in others? Is it not a heart of humility and of servanthood?

Who are the people you love and admire the most? Are they not the ones who give their lives for you like the great men and women of God who stand in power, but also stand as servants?

Well, how do you think they became such great leaders? By always being wonderful and magnificent?

No, they started out as servants! If the Lord has been putting some pressure on you in this area, then rejoice! You are right on track.

What does true servanthood forge in you? Firstly, it forces you to become reliable.

## 1. You Become Reliable

When you are forced to make sure the jobs are done on time, and the little things are taken care of, you become reliable.

When Craig and I are mentoring someone or training up a leader that is the first lesson we teach them. Very often when we mentor someone, they are living in our home. We give them responsibilities such as doing the garden, cleaning the pool, washing the dishes, and helping with the kids. We give them whatever job of servanthood we can find.

Why? So that I can have a housekeeper?

Sure, I appreciate the help, but it's because they need to learn to be reliable.

Let me tell you, I am tough! If the job is not done, I ask, "Excuse me, you haven't done this in a few days. Why is it not done?"

Sometimes you just need pressure put on you. The pressure of having to get the job done and the pressure of servanthood will make you reliable.

Once that pressure is lifted, you will find that you carry on serving. You carry on working hard. You carry on doing those things even in the higher position. *It puts a characteristic in you that you never had before.*

## 2. You Become Useful and Valuable

Think about it! If you fulfill a task so well that other people have liberty to do the work of the Lord, they will suffer without you there.

You are suddenly very useful. You are suddenly fulfilling a role and doing a job that is irreplaceable.

Perhaps you feel that this is unfair. Perhaps you want a place where you belong. You long to have a place that belongs to you alone and that no one else can take.

That is perfect. I can give you a place like that right now. Are you prepared to be a servant?

Are you prepared to be invaluable and reliable in the simple things? As you develop these leadership character traits, the Lord will continue to give you more responsibility until you are reliable and useful. It won't stop there though, because as you continue, you will learn to do greater tasks.

## Becoming a New Vessel

This first stage of leadership training breaks you down from being a molded vessel into becoming soft clay. Remember the vision of the clay pot being smashed that I shared with you earlier.

The smashing part is the first part, and also the toughest. Perhaps the person you have been up until now, was good enough for the job that was at hand. However, things have changed since then.

The Lord wants to use you in a higher capacity and for that to happen you need to become a different kind of vessel.

Unfortunately, we like to stick with the form that we have. We get used to the way we operate way too easily. We get comfortable in our own skin and when the Lord leads in a new direction, you are happy for Him to change the circumstances but not *you*.

### *For Circumstances to Change You Must Change*

Learn this lesson well! For circumstances to change, *you* must change! Do not think that people will suddenly start following you and that your ministry will take off while you remain stuck in your old form.

No, you must change! The Scripture says that there are vessels of honor and of dishonor in the house of the Lord. What kind of vessel do you want to be? If you want to be a vessel of honor, then obviously the vessel you are right now needs to change.

It is your fault, really. Do not complain to the Lord. You are the one who cried out with all of your breath pleading, "Use me, Lord!"

This smashing is His answer. Nothing smashes an old vessel better than a bit of old-fashioned humility. There is no humbler position than servanthood.

You crave respect and admiration. You want people to look up to you. However, you will keep going around the mountain until you come to the place where you no longer need these things.

You won't move beyond this point, until you are capable of serving in such a way that the Lord literally has to stop you from serving.

## How Do You Know When It Is Over?

The answer is simple. You will know that this stage is over when you can imagine yourself in that same place for years. When mowing the lawn is your favorite pastime and you could answer the phones forever, is likely the time the Lord will shift you into the second stage of your training.

When you are content to be in the background and don't care if people remember you, you will suddenly find yourself thrust forward.

When you come to the place of being proud of the fact that you can lift others up and make the leaders above you look good, those same leaders will suddenly lift you up in the sight of the people.

When your sole purpose is to serve and give others around you the opportunity to flow out in their ministry, you will find yourself on the stage giving out all God has for you.

The bottom line here really is that when you become content in your position of servanthood, a new door will be opened for you. It will come when you least expect it and you might even find yourself fighting it a little.

When this happens you know you are ready for stage two, the displacement phase of your training.

CHAPTER 14

# Second Stage of Leadership Training: Transformation Through Pressure

# Chapter 14 – Second Stage of Leadership Training: Transformation Through Pressure

I am no rocket scientist. In fact, truth be told, I am not an intellectual at all. I would rather hide behind the pulpit or spend my free time designing a new book cover.

For some reason though, the Lord would just not let me be. A new surprise waited for me when we took on the full load of A.M.I. Up until that point, my dad had programmed all of our websites.

He had worked in computer programming for years and without this skill, we would never have been able to reach the thousands that we did. Unfortunately though, things like that have to be maintained.

Who would do that now? Neither Craig nor I had a clue. I was really praying that the Lord would send someone with this knowledge.

He didn't.

So, we were stuck. We could not always run back to my dad and cry for help. He had so much on his own plate. One day he looked me squarely in the face and said, "Colette, there is no getting around it. You will need to learn this stuff."

I struggled. "Lord! This is not my thing. I am the artsy type. Give me something else to do."

The Scripture says that with every temptation given to man there is also given a way to escape. I started to wonder if this scripture applied to everyone else in the world except me.

I said, "Lord, where is my escape? I would like to run away from this one."

Nope. He was not going to let me hide. So, there was no choice. I just had to learn. It took me hours each day to start figuring out just what everything meant. This was really not my strength and each day I gave the Lord a short, sharp piece of my mind before begging Him for wisdom.

## No Way Out

The more I did it though, the more I started to learn. I started to develop a new character trait. Miss Expressive could be an intellectual after all!

Without the pressure of this situation, I would never have grown. That is why the second stage of training the Lord will take you through, is a phase filled with pressure situations.

When I say "pressure situation" I do not mean that He will lead you gently by the hand and show you where to go. No! I mean He will put you in the middle of a road, in the middle of the night, with nothing but a compass and flashlight and tell you to find your own way home.

Can you imagine how dramatic it must have been for Moses to go from 40 years alone time to leading millions of people? What a dramatic change.

He started the journey as one man and had transformed into another by the end. Had it not been for the pressure the Lord put on him, he would never have changed.

It was only when David faced Goliath that his calling really started. It was only after he had been wandering in the wilderness for a bit that he really learned to lead.

The same applies to you. It is going to take pressure to make you into the leader you need to become. So, if you have asked the Lord to lead you somewhere wonderful, expect him to put the pressure on you first to make you into something great.

Unless you become the right kind of person for the job, you cannot lead people to the place that they need to be in.

So, wait for it, because it is coming. Pressure! It is a vital phase of your training.

Servanthood is one thing, but pressure is another. The first stage of training strips you clean, but this stage adds to you. In the first stage it's as if the Lord takes everything from you that you thought you had only to give you things that you did not ask for in the second.

This is the most changing phase though and it is through this that you will transform.

You asked God for confidence, conviction and compassion. He answered by bring you pressure. Well, did you think the Lord would just walk up to you one day and slap it on your back?

I have never seen a diamond just form itself. No, it took pressure under the earth for years to forge it. This is also how a leader is made. It doesn't happen overnight, but they undergo a process of pressure that will force them to change.

## Why Is It Needed?

"Lord, please give me problems! Lord, please put pressures on me today to change me!" When was the last time you cried out to the Lord with such a prayer? No one likes pressure.

Instead you prayed, "Lord please give me your love. Lord, please make me confident." And so, the Lord looked at you and saw everything that stood in the way of this goal.

The Lord is doing is simply answering your prayer. Take notice of what He is saying! If you could change yourself, then you would not need the Lord.

If you were already a successful leader, then you would not be reading this book. However, you know you need to change! Are you willing to pay the price?

## Pressure for a Purpose

There is a reason that the pressure has been on you, but you have a choice to make here.

**Are you:**

a. Going to complain and have yourself a nice little pity party?
b. Going to embrace the pressure and change?

It is up to you really. You can either do this the hard way or the easy way. Each time you feel sorry for yourself and bewail how tough things are, you take a step down the ladder.

Each time you embrace the pressure that the Lord is throwing at you and submit to it, you take a step forward. This does not have to last forever. It is really up to you.

When you see that the pressure has a purpose, everything changes. You can embrace it because you realize the Lord is using it to change you.

## Different Forms of Pressure

Pressure can come in many forms. The Lord could start putting pressure on you using your marriage. He could start showing you that you have no love in your heart or that you do not know how to be vulnerable.

This pressure will also come through natural things. You will be forced to perform jobs you never could before.

The Lord might throw you into a situation where you have to be compassionate or care for people you never cared for before. If you have never worked with children before, He might throw you into a situation where you have to care of kids.

If you have always been behind the pulpit, He will throw you into personal ministry and vice versa.

He might suddenly load you with so much work that you feel you might be crushed under the weight of it all.

Wherever your weakness is, the Lord will apply pressure in that area until His strength starts to be forged in its place.

This means that you will be going through different pressure situations continually. The key is to identify the pressure.

So, think about it. What pressure situation are you in right now? What pressure did you face this week? Just think about the things that made you angry or uncomfortable.

Think about everything that you feel like running away from. Chances are that this is where the Lord is putting His finger right now.

My advice to you: Embrace it! Do not run from it but submit to that pressure and allow the Lord to use it to change you.

## 1. Displacement of Leadership Images

There is a method to this madness. Pressure will come on you for various reasons. I want to share some of the areas that I felt the Lord deal with in my own life.

As I go through them, I think you will find out that you are experiencing similar pressures.

All the wrong leadership images I had followed through the years, was the first thing the Lord started to show me as I began rising up. I can imagine that this was some of what David had to face as well.

He looked up to Saul so much that I wonder what kind of king he would have become had he not been forced out of the palace. It was only when David was in the wilderness that he saw Saul for the man he really was.

It was here that he could determine that he didn't want to become that same kind of king. His testing time came when the Lord led Saul right into David's hands.

Saul stood right in the cave within arm's reach. His men were saying, "Come on, David. You can do it! Kill him and take the throne!" In that moment David could have chosen to be like Saul. Saul would certainly not have thought twice about killing him.

I can imagine David wavering for that little moment, before saying, "No! I will not kill God's anointed." Right there he made a choice to become a different kind of leader to Saul. You will also be brought to this conviction.

You have not reached your goal as a leader yet, because of the wrong leadership images you have followed. There is no better way to deal with them though than going through some good pressure situations.

These pressures take you out of the situation and force you to look at them from afar. They force you to see the leaders you have followed in a new light. To clarify, I am not talking about the leaders you are angry at. I am talking about models that you have been following your whole life.

## Incorrect Parental Images

In fact, I suggest that you start with the leaders you admired while you were still in the crib. Yes, your parents! They were your first ever leaders, and you fashioned yourself after them.

What kind of leaders are your parents? Whether you like it or not, you would have taken on their image.

Then as you rose up and admired other people through life, you would have taken on their image too.

As the pressures come on you, you might find yourself thinking back on those leaders. You might even encounter crazy situations in which you think to yourself, "You know, as I do this, I can just imagine how my mother would have felt doing it," or ,"I feel just like my past mentor…"

When this happens, the Lord is trying to get your attention. He led you to the cave and put your Saul right in front of you. *What are you going to do?*

Will you be a leader like that person was, or will you take on a new mantle? Will you take on the image of Jesus?

The Lord will also bring you new images that are good for you to follow. Apostle Paul was not afraid to tell the churches to imitate him. He was a good image that they needed to follow.

As you go through this particular process, it will help you divide the good and bad leadership images you have followed.

## Correct Images of Past Mentors

It can be quite shocking when you realize that the Lord brought leaders into your life that you needed, but rejected! There were leaders in your past the Lord wanted you to learn from, but you either rejected them or got bitter.

On the other hand, you embraced other leaders you really should not have. As the pressures come on you, character traits, spiritual gifts, and anointings that you picked up along the way will be exposed.

So, consider where you are right now. As the pressure comes on you, what is it exposing inside of you? As you see what is being exposed, try and identify where you got that image from.

Where did you get that character trait from? Where did you get that strange habit from? Right here and now is the time for you to make a choice.

Will you continue in that way or will you let it go? You will go through an amazing transformation as the pressure exposes everything in you that is standing in the way of people following you.

You will be like David who looked back and saw others following him. So, dump the baggage! Allow the Lord to expose and get rid of all the junk you have carried all these years from parents, past mentors, and teachers.

Then allow Him to forge you into something wonderful and new.

## 2. Removing the Hindrances

I love the story of the man who carved an angel out of stone. Someone asked him, "How can you make such a beautiful angel?" He replied, "It's easy! All I do is take away the pieces that are not angel."

The same is true of the change the Lord takes us through. The Word says that He is the potter and we are the clay. Often the hindrances just have to be removed so that the good stuff in us can shine.

It was amazing when the Lord first revealed the principle of curses to us. Suddenly all of the finances we had been believing for started to pour in.

We learned that believing the Lord for finances had more to do with warfare than with begging Him. The Lord does not take forever to answer our prayers.

He wrote His promises in the Word and He does not change His mind. So, the blessing is there. The provision is there. Unfortunately though, we often get in the way of our own success. Our lack of faith and often also curses block the hand of God in our lives.

## Dealing With Curses

Remove the blockage and the blessing will flow. Remove the huge rock in the river that is blocking it and the water will flow again.

Growing up as a pastor's kid, I had no affection for the work of God. Surprised? Well, it was not that I did not love the Lord but the work of the ministry did not seem to be one of joy.

For me, serving the Lord meant always being poor and struggling along. Even though I had grown up and knew differently, somehow this thinking prevailed.

There had been so many in my family line who had tried ministry and failed. My own negative experiences only added to that. I am ashamed to admit it, but when we announced a seminar, I was expecting the people not to come!

How terrible is that? On the one hand I wanted to be used of the Lord, but on the other I struggled within myself. I had so many negative experiences.

The Lord used pressure situations to expose this. I realized that this was not only a curse in my life, but a very wrong expectation as well. How can I ask people to follow me on the one hand, but expect them not to on the other?

I had to change! I had to start with giving the Lord my bitterness towards the work of the ministry that I adopted when I was a child. Then I had to tell the enemy to take a hike. You won't believe the change I experienced!

We went from having to fight for every registration, to them coming in daily. As the pressures come on you, the Lord will not only expose the characteristics that must change, but any license that you have given to the enemy as well.

Perhaps you have already started to rise up as a leader. Perhaps the Lord has led people to you, but something keeps going wrong. You do not understand it! It's like you get so far and no further.

If you keep experiencing this, then maybe you have some curses operating in your life. Perhaps you have had so many negative experiences that you just do not want to expect good things anymore.

Perhaps out of everything, your greatest fear is being disappointed. On the one hand, you want to believe the Lord, but on the other you are afraid, in case everything falls apart.

Pressure situations are going to expose this thinking in you and then you'll have a choice to make. Will you commit your heart to this vision 100% or will you always hold a part of yourself back?

When Apostle Paul changed sides, he did not do it with any half measures. He gave himself over completely. I can imagine that he also had a lot of change to go through and mentors to let go of.

How do I know this? Paul says that he was a student of the great Gamaliel. He was a respected Pharisee of the highest order. Do we see Paul following in his footsteps?

Quite the opposite is true, actually. He started out trying to reach his own people, but faced one closed door after the other. After giving it his best shot, he and Barnabus finally got the message. Instead of pushing "against the pricks", he embraced the pressure and said, "It was necessary that we spoke to you first but seeing as though you do not receive our word, we are going to the Gentiles!"

This was a far cry from the image his old mentor had given to him. He turned around completely and went against everything he had been taught to start a revolution in the church.

Paul did not have it easy by any means. The church was not sure of him and the Jews hated him. From the time Jesus visited him with a bright shining light, Paul experienced one pressure after the other.

## What the Second Stage Forges in You

I have worked with people who had a real servant's heart and were prepared to let go of their identity. They let go of their titles, got down on their knees and mopped the floors with their bare hands because there was nothing else to use.

They have now risen up and launched to the top of the ladder to stand as apostles, as leaders in the Kingdom of God.

### 1. It Qualifies You

If Jesus Christ, the Son of God, could throw aside His crown and mantle and get down on His hands and knees to wash His disciples' feet, who are you to want to bypass that whole phase of training?

You can't have the glory without paying the price. *You can't have the title without letting it go first.*

Perhaps you feel as if you are going around in circles right now. Nothing seems to be happening with your vision. Have you excelled in servanthood?

Have you taken everything you could from the pressure situations God put you into? Did you learn everything that you could during that time? Did you serve with joy and then ask for more?

You are the first to notice that a mess was spilled, and jump up to clean it. Although no one else noticed, you were the one to give up your seat for someone else.

You are the first one to offer help to others when no one else wants to step forward.

Let me tell you, if you have been faithful in this, you will be the first person they will call if anybody has a problem.

When they are thinking of someone to spend time with, guess who they will call? When they are thinking of people they are most grateful for, guess who they will think of?

You can apply this principle in the workplace and in the world just as much as in the Church. The people who are prepared to do the low things, will also have the confidence to stand up and do the higher things.

## 2. You Become Capable With New Skills

As a trainer, a lot of my time is spent working with people, teaching them how to do things.

Before they can help me with any task in the ministry, I have to train them into it. So, I spend time training them and so they learn new skills all the time.

I am not just talking about spiritual things here either. I am talking about teaching them how to do the dishes, write admin letters, handle sound equipment, or set up lighting.

As they learn, they become useful and more importantly, they become valuable.

Look at your life and think about the times when you were pushed into a certain direction and had pressure put on you to learn something new.

It might not have been comfortable, but you learned something new. Through that you added a new skill to your list of qualities.

Can you see the value of this? It makes you knowledgeable. You learn things you never did before. The more you learn, the more you become irreplaceable.

Everybody wants to be irreplaceable. You want to think that there is only one of you in the world and that no one can take your place.

Do you realize though that this can only take place if you are a true servant?

## 3. You Become Valuable

Consider the story of Joseph when he worked for Potiphar and his wife. You read how Potiphar could leave his whole household in Joseph's care. He didn't even have to care about it.

Wow! What a valuable man. He was so valuable that the owner could step away for days. Unfortunately, he left Joseph alone with his wife, but that's another story...

Joseph was so valuable to Potiphar that he could leave his home for days and not have a care in the world.

We know how the story goes. After the situation with Potiphar's wife, Joseph gets thrown into prison.

Just consider this for a moment. He is a prisoner, thrown in jail with a bunch of criminals! The Scripture says that the warden didn't even have to check up on Joseph because he knew that everything would be taken care of.

He was a prisoner! Yet he became so valuable and useful that the warden didn't even check up on him. We can see how the traits that were built into him during the seasons of servanthood and pressure, are beginning to show themselves.

## From Servant to King

These very circumstances wrought in him everything he needed to rise up as the second in command in all of Egypt!

That servanthood training and the pressure he faced equipped him to become a great leader. Whatever situation you are facing right now, realize that God is forging something in you.

As you asked Him to become a leader, He is taking you through the pressure situations you need, to make you into something you are not right now.

The Scripture is full of examples. Look at Samuel. He was dropped off at Eli's door at around three years of age. He started out as nothing but a little servant boy in his little linen ephod.

He proceeded to rise up to become one of Israel's greatest judges and was responsible for anointing two kings.

Not only did he become valuable to the Lord through his season of servanthood, but he became valuable to the children of Israel as well.

Do you want to be irreplaceable and unique? This is going to secure your place.

*It is not about what a great leader you are. It is about what kind of servant you are.*

*It is not about how many things you can do, but how many things you are still willing to do.*

Depending on what kind of servant you are and how much pressure you are willing to embrace, I can look at you and determine what kind of leader you will become.

## Look at Our Examples

### David

A little shepherd boy working in the courts of Saul, yet the greatest King who ever lived.

### Joshua

He served at Moses' side as his bodyguard and servant. Yet he took over the position of leading the whole congregation of Israel into the Promised Land.

### Elisha

He washed the hands of Elijah, yet rose up with double of Elijah's anointing.

All of the great men and women in the Word had something in common.

They all started out washing hands, cleaning floors, caring for sheep, and taking the lower seat. They all started out as nobodies.

Suddenly your situation does not look so bad anymore.

**Moses**

Consider poor Moses, taking care of Jethro's stinky goats out in the wilderness. Just wonderful! I can think of better things to do on my Saturday afternoon… how about you?

## 4. You Qualify to Start Leading

More importantly, you will be equipped to pass what you learned onto others. You will become qualified to train others to be leaders.

It will be you training others to do things like cooking, cleaning, writing, ministering, and leading.

Unless you have done those things yourself first, you cannot stand up and say, "This is the way things should be done!"

How can you train others to be good believers in every area of their lives, if you haven't learned it yourself? It begins with being an example and this example is forged by going up the ranks a step at a time.

## Your Next Step

Take a look at your situation. You asked the Lord to use you and I guarantee that God has opened the way for you to die.

He will open the way for you to serve and to be humbled. So, stop whining but see what He has done. He is giving you the opportunity to gain real leadership traits.

Has He perhaps put you in the home of a family? Perhaps you feel that they just expect too much of you. If this is the case, then give more than what they ask for.

Find opportunities to serve! Find things to do! Put yourself in the place of always being the first to answer, the first to do, and the first to try.

This will equip you. It will forge character in you. It will put pressure on you to change.

I really cannot emphasize the power of this training enough. It is the foundation of your leadership.

If you want to be a leader who rises up high, then start down low.

Then you will come to the place where you are so comfortable with serving and learning, it has become second nature. You will be the first to offer a helping hand to anyone.

When you come to that place of being settled and you even, dare I say, enjoy it, God will open the way.

Just as he opened the way for Joshua, Joseph, and Elisha, He will also open the way for you.

I think Joseph might have been stubborn because it took him many years to learn his lessons. It doesn't have to take you that long.

God will open the way for you, but you will look back on those days and miss them. You will miss the times of just being a little quieter, and of not having to carry the responsibility of leadership.

When the season comes to an end you will think back on it with fond memories. You will remember what God did in you through this time.

Do you want the higher positions in the world or in the Church? Do you want to be launched up the leadership ladder? Then be the first to give.

Be the first to complete the task. Be the first to take the lower seat. Be the first to raise others up. Then you will also be the first God uses.

# CHAPTER 15

# Third Stage of Leadership Training: Taking on the Load

# Chapter 15 – Third Stage of Leadership Training: Taking on the Load

Nothing quite prepares you when you taking on the load of leadership for the first time all by yourself. You can read a library of books and study as much self-help as you like, but nothing compares to doing the stuff.

It feels a lot like traveling to a new country. I have experienced this many times but I still find myself surprised and astounded.

My greatest culture shock though was the time we went to Switzerland. We had been invited to help with a work there. So, we packed up our kids and landed there late in the afternoon.

It was winter and had been snowing quite a lot. I had never seen snow in my life before and so this winter wonderland was something out of a book for me.

The more we traveled, the more I felt like Dorothy in the Wizard of Oz. We were NOT in "Kansas" anymore.

Everything was drastically different to what we knew. The roads were small and narrow. The architecture was completely different. Stores closed for lunch and the winding mountain roads terrified me.

We arrived at the home we would stay in and everything seemed so tiny. We were tired, missing our family, and everything was coming at us all at once.

Our hosts left us, and I was on the verge of having an all fall down. What did it for me was the toilet! How complicated could it be to just use the bathroom?

It took me a good 15 minutes to figure out how to flush it. That was me! Here I was… falling apart over a toilet.

Silly, isn't it? When you are thrust onto the unknown road of leadership, many surprises are waiting for you. It does not even matter how much you prepare. There is no better way to learn these things than to live them.

That is why the most important and ongoing phase of your leadership training is the last one. In this phase you learn about leadership on the go.

I can imagine Moses learned a thing or two on the road to the Promised Land. The idea seemed all wonderful as he boldly approached Pharaoh, but when they faced their first obstacle and the people wanted water, things got difficult for him.

A bit at a time though, he learned to be that leader. Not only did he lead the children of Israel to the Promised Land, but he also produced the first five books of our bible. That is not a bad accomplishment indeed.

The greatest part of your journey stands in front of you in the great unknown. If you like to play it safe, you could trip yourself up right here.

Sorry. There is no easy way around this. You can only walk through it. You will only understand the lessons when you live them and map out the road when you walk it.

## Taking on the Load of Responsibility

Having traveled this road a bit ahead of you, I can give you a few things to look for along the way. I can offer you some of my "toilet flushing" counsel and give you some "how not to panic when it happens to you" words of comfort.

However, the road is yours to walk. As you take each step, watch the journey unfold. Learn each lesson that comes at you. Embrace each pressure and through it you will find people following you. Furthermore, when you look in the mirror you will see someone who is starting to resemble the image of Christ.

## Forget the Duckies

The first thing we all like to do when facing a task is what I call "getting all your duckies in a row." That term comes from the picture of the mother duck leading the way as her little brood follows on after in a neat, straight line.

We like things neatly organized and to have a clear idea of what we want out of our vision.

The first thing I learned when I took the load of leadership is that you are not at the helm of this ship, but the Lord is. Consider Moses who led the people following the pillar of cloud and fire.

He did not make up his own plan. He knew where he was leading them and he also knew what he was offering them. How he got there though, was entirely up to the Lord.

You can get so busy trying to figure out how to get to your destination that at times you can plan the Lord right out of it. You see, I have always loved training people. It was my passion.

I figured that if Craig and I were to grow A.M.I. that it would happen through the sole application of training. Wrong move! I was telling God what to do with the ministry. I came to find out quite quickly that the training aspect of our ministry was just that, an aspect.

## Your Vision Will Unfold

The Lord had an entire vision that I didn't think about. Now that you have a clear idea of where you want to take the people, I am here to tell you that a few surprises are waiting for you up ahead.

What the children of Israel did not know was that a mountain would be a detour along their journey. They did not know that they would get to see the Almighty God. Moses did not know that he would receive the law and certainly could not imagine that he would see Almighty God Himself.

These things unfolded along the journey and you should be prepared to follow in the Lord's footsteps. You will soon come to realize that this ministry and vision is not your own, but that it belongs to the Lord.

So, make sure that it stays in His ownership. The minute you take things into your own hands, prepare yourself for a nasty idol worshipping incident followed by the bitter taste of that idol crushed in water.

Keep God at the helm. Let Him direct your cloud and fire! You simply follow. Follow when it makes sense but follow especially when it does not make sense.

How much sense did it make to come face-to-face with the Red Sea? God saw a bigger plan and that crazy route drowned the Egyptians. This is where we differ so much from the world.

The Lord will lead you in surprising directions that people might not understand. It is at times like these when your faith in the Lord has to be stronger than your faith in yourself. Your faith in Him must be stronger than your doubt or fear.

Your love for the Lord has to be stronger than your need for the love of the people. When the Lord is the center of your direction, you will always find your feet on steady ground.

## Seems Like Too Much at First

The first thing you might experience is feeling like the whole ordeal is a bit much. Similar to the 2$^{nd}$ stage of training, pressures will come at you from all sides.

You will have new decisions to make and it is quite a job being responsible for others. If things do not go well, then they suffer. This is especially true when people are dependent on you for finances or daily needs.

You can choose to react to the pressure by running away or you can face it. If you have passed through the other stages of training correctly, then you will be ready to face it. However, a bit of humility goes a long way.

I would rather walk into a situation with caution than be so arrogant and think that I can handle anything that is thrown at me. Rather be open for correction and to learn. A good leader knows the boundaries of their strengths and weaknesses.

Do not rush into a situation and think that just because you are the leader you can handle it. Use caution and walk with wisdom. Soon enough the things that seemed so difficult at the beginning will feel comfortable.

Some people get the idea that you land fully grown in a leadership position. It is not true though. It is something that you grow into.

## Growing Into Your Position

It took Moses something like 80 years before he took on his load and it took Joshua probably just as long! It took them a while to grow into their positions.

David was a young king, but it took him a good few years after being anointed before he was ready.

In fact, before he took on the throne entirely, the Lord had grace on him. He gave him Judah for a couple of years first. Saul, on the other hand, was lumped with the entire load and it just about crippled him.

He bowed under pressure and did rather what the people said than what God wanted. With David it was different. He was given a bit more time to grow into the position.

Solomon had David around for a while before taking on the responsibility all by himself. This made for a wise King who did not rush into anything but followed the wisdom of the Lord.

So, do not rush in with guns blazing. Keep your ear firmly to the Lord's chest and make full use of the leadership position that you are in right now.

## Under Another Leader

Are you an assistant pastor or an assistant in someone else's ministry? If so, how are you using this position to grow? Are you being wise with it like David and Joshua were or are you complaining, just wanting your own big break?

What you do not realize is that the Lord is giving you an opportunity to learn in a safe environment first. So, stop kicking and screaming and learn the lessons that you can. Be like David who was patient enough to wait. As a result, he eventually took on the throne with full honors!

He did not have to wage war for it. In fact, when the time came, the generals looked for him and took him as their king. So, bide your time and learn what you are supposed to be learning right now.

I can tell you that unless you learn what God put you there for, you won't move beyond this point.

Do you always find yourself as the assistant instead of the guy in charge? Then you have not learned your lesson yet. You have not learned yet what God is trying to show you. Learn what you can! Rise up where you can!

Become valuable and embrace the pressures. Once you have passed those tests, you will be ready to step into something new.

# Testing Time Begins

It is one thing to handle pressure from a boss and another to handle it from circumstances and the people around you. When you are under another leader, you might not like what they say, but you have to submit.

It is tough and if you are wise, you will take what they say into account. You will use that pressure to change you.

However, what happens when you are the boss, when you are the "buck"? I said to one of my trainees after I had to apply a correction in their training, "There is only one thing worse than receiving a correction from your mentor and that is not having a mentor to receive a correction from."

You think it would be so nice not to have someone there to boss you around. I can imagine that after just a few incidents with the Israelites Moses would have gone back to his father-in-law anytime!

Take a good look at Jesus on the cross and you will get an idea of the kind of pressures you will face when you are the leader. Do you remember all those bad attitudes you had about other leaders?

Do you remember all that good advice you thought you would give your leaders?

Well, welcome home! Now you have a bunch of people all around you thinking just like you did.

They are questioning your moves and wondering why you did what you did. You have your own Aarons and Miriams now to question your decisions.

These are the making and breaking times that will decide if you will rise up in your leadership or fall flat on your face.

## Not to Respond in Bitterness

The temptation to get bitter in response to people rejecting or standing against you, will be the first test you need to face. After all, it was you who birthed this vision. It was you who came up with the ideas.

It is so easy for them to talk, when you did all the work! Does this sound familiar to you? How did Moses deal with his rejections? Did he curse Miriam? No, he let the Lord handle the situation.

When Adonijah tried to take the throne from Solomon, it was his mother and the priest who ran to David to sort it out. He did not have to defend himself. That only came later as he got established.

If you respond in anger and bitterness, you will undo everything that you have started.

Let's say you have someone in your team who is driving you nuts. They question and challenge you.

Does this mean you kick them out? Or, could it perhaps be that you have someone just like you on board?

How would you like to have been handled? Think about the last leaders you were under. How did you treat them?

## The Penny Drops

When I gave birth to my first child, I suddenly had an appreciation for what my mother went through for me. When my daughters started to enter their teen years, I felt a sudden compassion for the gray hairs I gave my own father.

It is no different with you. You were hardly a saint as you were finding your way. When you start to look at people through these eyes, it gives you compassion.

It also releases the greatest power of all… the power of love! You can both correct and motivate them, having love as your anchor.

If you respond in bitterness, you will only push them away. Also, do not forget, this is a phase of training.

I can guarantee that some of the first challenges you will face will dig things out of your flesh you never knew were there. You will react with emotions that had been buried your entire life.

It is very easy to lead when everyone is nice to you. What happens when they stop being nice to you? That is when the real training kicks in.

You will be opposed, and you will be challenged. The question is, how will you respond to these things?

"Well, I am the boss here, you just have to submit!" Will that be your response or will you use wisdom and what God is telling you?

Moses got it both right and wrong. When the people complained instead of getting bitter, he ran to the Lord. They pushed him just too far once though. They were grumbling yet again because of water and he got hopping mad.

The Lord told him to talk to the rock and the water would come, but instead he struck it.

The Lord was angry with him and it was because of this that the Lord said he would not enter the Promised Land. When the people grumble, how are you reacting?

Are you getting angry and bitter? Are you justifying yourself? Or, are you allowing these pressures to shape you?

## Rejection and Opposition

Life is not fair. Embrace it and move on. Only then will you truly rise up. If you expect everyone to love you along with everything that you do, then I am afraid you decided on the wrong course of action.

The people who loved Jesus were not the ones who had power at that time. The ones who had the power hated Him and dragged Him to the cross.

Jesus knew it would happen. Did He shy away from that pressure? No, He knew that the greatest power lay beyond the cross and although it was not easy, He embraced it. As a result, His work continues to thrive today.

Can the same be said of you? What happened the last time people came against you? What was your reaction? Instead of trying to change them, why don't you stop and see what God is trying to change in you?

Each time you adopt this attitude, you will gain a new character trait.

This final stage will breed skills and character traits in you that were completely foreign to you before. If you lacked patience before, then you will learn it.

If you lacked the ability to plan before, then this phase will force you into it. You will be challenged to change temperaments and become all things to all men.

The good news is that this is not an instant change. This is not one of those "just add water and stir recipes." This is a gradual process and the Lord will continue to add to you over time.

## Will You Ever Arrive?

Well... do you want to? I sure hope that I never get to the place where I say, "Now I am the best leader I could ever be!" How about you?

Even as I came to write this book I struggled with the Lord. I said, "Lord, how can I teach on the subject of leadership when I still have so much to learn myself?"

The Lord told me to teach what I know so far. You see, the process is ongoing. There is always a new mountain to climb and a new glory to enter into.

How do I know that? Well, the Word says that we are changed continually through the agency of the Holy Spirit into the image of Christ from glory to glory.

Do you look like Jesus yet? If you don't then you are not there yet. That is your final goal. We still have another glory to go to before you and I resemble Jesus in all His grace and love.

## 1. Your Mountain Experience

The greatest change you will experience in your final stage of training won't be in front of the masses. It won't be as you lead your team, or make your 100$^{th}$ decision before your morning cup of coffee.

The greatest change will come in your time on the mountain. When Jesus was with the Father on the mount of transfiguration, Matthew 17:2 says that His face shone like the sun.

Do you remember someone else who had a similar experience? You got it! It was Moses. After he had seen the Lord's afterglow, he came down the mountain and he glowed with the glory.

Through all those years and all his experiences, the greatest change he went through was in that moment in the presence of the Father. This is where you will also learn to change.

You can only receive so much change in the natural. Natural pressures from around you can only shape your character so much.

Sooner or later you will come to experience something that I once did. You will come to the end of your resources.

## The Only Place Left to Hide

It won't matter anymore how much you submit to the pressures. It won't matter how hard you try. It won't matter how much you submit. You will eventually cry out like I did, "Lord, it is not enough! I cannot do it."

When you finally come to this point, I dare say your real journey finally begins. The greatest lesson of all is that change comes from within.

All those pressures have brought you to a place of realizing how much you need help. They have allowed you to see what a leader you are not.

They have exposed your sin and your flaws. They have put a spotlight on your weakness and inability.

You can only change so much in yourself. It seems the Lord knew that! It is why Jesus came in the first place. He knew that we were limited in what we could do. We needed a Savior and He came to save you from a lot more than just your sin.

*He came to save you from yourself.*

## 2. New DNA From the Father

From the moment you were conceived in your mother's womb you have been conditioned for life. Every circumstance you have faced and every teacher you have had has shaped your mind, emotions, and will.

Everything you learned became a foundation for where you are now. Have you ever wondered why some people find it easy to lead and others do not?

Have you ever wondered why some find it so easy to get rich and others do not? Take a good look at both spiritual and soul DNA.

Just like natural DNA makes up the building blocks of what gives us our eye color or gender, so also does soul DNA make up why we believe what we do. It makes up why you act the way that you do.

All of this did not just form in you overnight. As a baby, you were a clean slate but you just took everything that came at you. You didn't know any better. Unfortunately though, not everything that was written on that clean slate destined you for success.

And so here you are, struggling with yourself just like Paul did. You are crying out to the Lord saying, "Lord! Help me here! I know what I should be doing, but I do not do it. I know that I should be doing good, but I do bad instead. I am struggling with a war inside of me."

What you need is a work of God. When Jesus died, He didn't just save you from your sin, but He also gave you the power to really change! He gave you the power to rewrite some of that slate that has been written on over the years.

Have you ever heard the term "to have the mind of Christ?" Well, that is a study in itself, but what you need to do right now is to start seeing things as God sees them.

You need to see your situation as God sees it. You need to do what God would do. You need to think like Jesus! So how will you do that?

Well, how did a baby learn to think like its mother? It was just born to her. In the same way you have been born again and you have been given a clean slate.

You can ask the Lord to come and write His DNA on that slate. You can ask Him to show you what to read and what to pray. More importantly though, you can ask Him to come and displace the way you view life with His power.

It is as miraculous as a physical healing and it is something that only comes from being in His presence. Moses learned to see things God's way.

The Lord said that He spoke to Moses face-to-face. The Lord shaped the way Moses thought and did things. He can do the same for you.

He can undo your poverty mentalities and your fears of the future. He can give you a fresh perspective on how to handle people, and a fresh revelation on how to walk your road.

It does not come independently from Him though. Moses' face only glowed after being in the presence of the Father. The same rings true for you.

Take time to shut yourself away with the Lord. Hear His voice and follow His direction. Feed on His word and let him change the way you think.

Faith comes by hearing and hearing by the rhema word of God. If you are not hearing the rhema word of God, how will you be changed?

The Word says that our minds should continually be transformed and renewed. How do you think that will happen? It will happen as you hear the Lord's voice and read His Word.

## Taking on His DNA

When you do this, He will show you what to read and where to go. Then He will give you confirmation of these things and speak with you face-to-face.

The more you follow Him and listen to Him, the more that DNA inside of you will start to transform. The entire concept of spiritual and soulish DNA is a massive subject and we published many materials on this. So consider this just a touch on it.

My point is that *to do great works, you need a great God.* To see things from a new perspective, you need to see through God's eyes. To have the mind of Christ, you need to receive it from the one to whom it belongs.

Your greatest change will happen on the top of the mountain and it is only here that your leadership will be tried and proven by the Holy Spirit Himself.

## Doing It in His Power

It will take a lot more than skills and ability to make you a leader like Christ. It will take a lot more than a good personality to keep people following you.

Sure, you can decide to take these principles and use them to become a worldly leader. A lot of what I have shared in this book can be applied to all kinds of leadership.

What I have taught you on handling the public or people close to you, works on believers and unbelievers alike. So, what is it that you really wanted to learn as you picked up this book?

Did you want people to follow you so that your name could be high and lifted up, or did you read it so that Jesus could be high and lifted up?

I have shared things I have learned along the way and I know that there are those who will take these principles and make them work for their own end.

I hold onto the hope though that you are one of those who have a hunger for the Lord. I pray that you love the Lord Jesus more than you love your own recognition.

## One Final Principle

If you are one of those, then I have one final principle for you. It will take everything you have learned so far and multiply it so much so that you will rise up higher than all the other leaders around you.

When you take the natural principles I have taught and you take the common sense I have advised you with, you could become a pretty good leader.

However, if you take all that and add the power of the Holy Spirit to it, you get a *Jesus kind of leader*. You get a Moses who can part the Red Sea. You get a Joshua who can stop the earth in its orbit.

You get a David who can leap over a wall. You get a Solomon who can walk in divine wisdom. You get the kind of leader history is made of. If you want to be a little more than the average leader, then you need to remember that the core of your leadership is made up of the power of Christ.

Jesus paid one hefty price to make His power available to us. In the Old Testament, saints had to wait for the mercy of God. The Lord picked out a few and only they experienced His power.

However, Jesus changed all that. From the time He rose again, He gave all of us that same power. That is why it surprises me so much that there are so many out there who prefer to use their natural abilities, leaving the Lord's power out of it.

I guess it is a mixed up thinking in the Church. They have separated leadership from the anointing. They have separated good management from their calling.

God is calling forth a new era of leaders in this day and age and I invite you to join the ranks. They are leaders who are humble in themselves and confident in the Lord.

They are leaders who don't just know their limitations and weaknesses, but glory in them, so that the strength of the Lord can shine through them.

They are leaders who would rather take the anointing than hold onto the approval of the masses. They are leaders like Moses, David, Peter, and Jesus.

It is time we saw leaders like that rise up. Do not be afraid to stand up and be counted, because it is time that the Church enters into its Promised Land.

It will take committed leaders who know where they are going to lead them.

It will take anointed leaders who have the tools to get them there.

It will take obedient leaders who can follow the cloud and map out the right route.

It will take leaders like Jesus and together we will surely transform the Church and this world. Then the Church will be as a city on a hill and it will shine for miles and miles.

Never forget that the Lord will raise you up and that there are many who will follow you. When this happens, know that it is not because of you, but because of Him.

## Why You Will Succeed

After a few years of carrying the full load of the ministry, the blessing of the Lord started flowing. There was a temptation in me to say, "Wow! Look at how well we are doing. We must be doing something right."

However, the Lord humbled me and said so clearly, "It is not because of you that things are going right, but because of me. I need the resources that you have for my Bride. I need to use you as a vessel for my work and that is why I am prospering you."

I felt like Moses on my face before Him. All the doors He opened and all the work He did was not about our great skill.

All of the blessing and success had nothing to do with how well we had passed the tests. At the end of the day, we were a vessel that God needed to use. We were suddenly in the right place at the right time for Him to do what He wanted.

So, child of God, when you finally come to that place when your foot lands itself on your Promised Land, know this:

You walk this road because of His grace.

You take this land because of His power.

You walk through this door because of His plan.

People will follow you for one reason alone: to show forth the glory of God.

## Final Prayer

No matter where you are right now, I want to stand in agreement with you and speak the will of the Lord over your life. Reach out by faith and commit yourself to the road ahead.

It is for the Lord to open the doors. All that is left for you to do is walk through them.

Thank you, Holy Spirit, for your power and your presence. Lord, we commit to the road ahead. I look at the door that is ahead in the spirit and I thank you that it is time now for it to open!

## Calling Forth the Pillars of Fire

For you have indeed walked a long journey, says the Lord, and I have brought you to such a time as this. As you have traveled many roads of many kinds, now is the time for you to walk a new road with intent.

For you will find that the many roads lead up to this single road and as I open the doors in front of you, there will be no going back.

For it is indeed time for my Church to take the land that I have promised. It is indeed time for my mighty warrior to rise up and to take back by force what the enemy has stolen.

And so, it is time to rise up! However, I need my leaders to wake my Church from her slumber. I need my leaders to equip her. I need my leaders to go ahead.

I need leaders who are not afraid to face the storms, to go a way no one has gone before, and to pay the price for others to walk.

I need leaders who will walk the roads and learn them, who will write the map and then lead others along the way. For I am raising up mighty warriors even now, says the Lord. I am bringing them forth from all points in the earth and they will take their place.

Then I will surely set them on fire and together they will set my Church ablaze. For it is time for all of my leaders to come from all over, to join as a mighty force to lead. I shall surely give them the same spirit and the same fire.

They will identify one another by this fire. For I am indeed bringing a mighty move to my body, says the Lord, and I shall do it over the entire world. I will not start a fire here or a fire there, but I shall start it as one.

Have I said it, and shall I not do it? Shall I not do what I have promised for generations to do, my child? So, take my hand and join me as I raise these ones up.

For the time is short and the training has been long. Each must let go of what comforts them and each must let go of what they know. They must let go so that I can give them my mind and my fire.

For this is indeed my Bride and I shall breathe over her and I shall use the vessels that I choose. So, look up and be prepared, says the Lord, for a mighty wave is coming and it shall come through those that I raise up to stand as pillars of fire, says the Lord. Amen.

# About the Author

Born in Bulawayo, Zimbabwe and raised in South Africa, Colette had a zeal to serve the Lord from a young age. Coming from a long line of Christian leaders and having grown up as a pastor's kid, she is no stranger to the realities of ministry. Despite having to endure many hardships such as her parents' divorce, rejection, and poverty, she continues to follow after the Lord passionately. Overcoming these obstacles early in her life has built a foundation of compassion and desire to help others gain victory in their lives.

Since then, the Lord led Colette, with her husband, Craig Toach, to establish *Apostolic Movement International* and *Toach Ministries International*

*Apostolic Movement International* focuses on training those called to the fivefold ministry whereas *Toach Ministries International* ministers to, covers, supports, and spiritually parents like-minded leaders.

In addition, Colette is a fantastic cook, an amazing mom to not only her four natural children, but to her numerous spiritual children all over the world. Colette is also a renowned author, mentor, trainer, and a woman that has great taste in shoes! The scripture to "be all things to all men" definitely applies to her, and the Lord keeps adding to that list of things each and every day.

How does she do it all? Experience through every book and teaching the life of an apostle firsthand and get the insight into how the call of God can make every aspect of your life an incredible adventure.

# Other Books by Colette Toach

If you enjoyed this book, I know you will also love the following books.

## The Apostolic Handbook

**Your Personal Voyage to Apostolic Office**

ISBN: 978-1-62664-015-3

This book has the potential to not only confirm your calling, but to launch you headfirst into the training that will take you to apostolic office.

If you have the suspicion or the strong conviction that you have been called to be an apostle, then you are in for the adventure of a lifetime. In fact, you hold in your hands a treasure map that gives you clear directions.

## Practical Prophetic Ministry

**The Metamorphosis of the Prophet**

ISBN: 978-1-62664-017-7

Wouldn't it be incredible if someone could have walked you through your prophetic calling and pointed out all the potholes before you fell into them?

Unfolded step by step, you will have someone along the way telling you what to avoid, what to embrace, and most importantly... what to do next along your prophetic journey.

## Persistent Prayer

**Angels and Demons at Work**

ISBN: 978-1-62664-225-6

Prayer is our connection to the Lord. It takes the will of God in heaven and brings it down to the earth. It removes the hindrances that stand in the way, allows man to hear God, and blocks the enemy completely! When you couple this with someone who is ready to speak, obey, and do the will of God in this earth, you get a recipe for a highly successful prayer life.

## Mentorship 101

**Bringing Out the Treasure in God's People**

ISBN: 978-1-62664-067-2

Mentorship! What picture comes into your mind? It is a very hot topic in the church today, but clear teaching is lacking. In this series, you will not only find out what the role and purpose of a mentor is, but you will see the heart that is required!

God is raising up His mighty warrior, and if you want to be on the front lines of equipping God's people, this series will show you how!

# Further Recommendations by the Author

## Earn a Diploma That Truly Validates Your Call

With over twenty years' experience in full-time ministry, Apostles Craig and Colette Toach know the fire that burns in you to do the work of God.

How to Get People to Follow You

With a focus on spiritual parenting, mentorship, and hands-on training, each school equips you to do the work of God. Consider us boot camp for your fivefold ministry call.

Each course is video based with required report submissions for you to complete after each lesson. Each student is allocated a trainer who marks all reports, follows up with personal ministry, and laying on of hands at graduation.

## AMI Prophetic School:

www.prophetic-school.com

There is a clear track that the Holy Spirit follows to train up His prophets. Having trained prophets into office all over the world, your calling will find itself in an environment where your prophetic mandate is as important to us as it is to you.

Think: training, impartation, and mentorship. By the time you walk the stage at your graduation, you would have done more than just studied for a diploma – you would have embarked on a journey that would have equipped you to fulfill your mandate as a prophet in office.

## AMI Pastor Teacher School:

www.pastorteacherschool.com

Everything you wish you knew about doing the work of the ministry. Our student complement consists of pastors, ministry leaders, apostles, and various fivefold ministers who crave a deeper reality of the Lord and their calling.

With an emphasis on becoming equipped, each course gears you towards functioning in a leadership capacity. Whether that is behind the pulpit or in a home church setting, you will receive training that by the time you walk the stage, would have already geared you towards apostolic ministry.

## AMI Campus:

www.ami-campus.com

Not ready to commit to a lengthy training program? No problem! You are welcome to study independently and pick and choose between prophetic, pastoral, teaching, and apostolic courses that tailor fit you right where you are at.

The main difference between our public campus and our other schools is that associates in our campus do not graduate, but rather join a family of like-minded believers. Every associate is supported by qualified pastors and guided through their individual training process. We are here to see your process through!

**Colette Toach's books are now available on both, Kindle**

**and iBooks!**

# Reach out!

Find out More Here:
www.colette-toach.com

Connect with Colette Toach on Facebook!
www.facebook.com/ColetteToach

Check Colette out on Amazon.com at:
www.amazon.com/author/colettetoach

Connect with Craig and Colette Toach Personally:
www.toach-ministries.com


Get Colette's books at AMI Bookshop: www.ami-bookshop.com

**Telephone**: +1 (760) 466 - 7679

(9am to 5pm California Time, Tuesday – Saturday)

**E-mail Address**: admin@ami-bookshop.com

# Bibliography

Toach, Colette. *Practical Prophetic Ministry: The Metamorphosis of the Prophet.* 3rd ed. San Diego, California: Apostolic Movement International LLC, 2016

Toach, Colette. *The Crucified Life*. MP3 file. San Diego, California: Apostolic Movement International LLC, 2015

Toach, Colette. *The Way of Dreams and Visions: Interpreting Your Secret Conversion with God.* 3rd ed. San Diego, California: Apostolic Movement International LLC, 2016